The Complete Book of Household Lists

Nina Grunfeld

PIATKUS

Other books by the author:

World's Work
Spot Check, how to cope with household stains, with Michael Thomas.

Ballantine Books
2001 Gifts, a sensational catalog of gift ideas.

© 1982 Nina Grunfeld

First published in 1982 by Judy Piatkus (Publishers) Limited of Loughton, Essex.

British Library Cataloguing in Publication Data

Grunfeld, Nina
  The complete book of household lists.
  1. Home economics – handbooks, manuals, etc.
  I. Title
  640   TX159

  ISBN 0-86188-170-2

Designed by Andrew Roberts and Nina Grunfeld.

Jacket designed by Richard Garratt.

Typeset by Tradespools Limited, Frome, Somerset.

Printed and bound by Mackays of Chatham.

Contents

You

Acknowledgements

With thanks to David Tilly (Home); Pickfords Removals Ltd (Moving); Tony Wilkins from *Do It Yourself* magazine (Decorating); my mother (Cleaning); Sara Harvey (Eating); Andy Quartermaine (Safety); Frank (Transport); Jane Lowmass (Gardening); P. A. Stevens from the seed shop in Covent Garden (Gardening); Dr Alison Groves (health, and holiday expertise); Rosalyn Kennedy (Clothes); Katrina Barnicoat (Family); Carolyn and Beth (Family); Judith Hill from *Mother* magazine (Family); Nick Van Veen (Pets, and lots of gardening hints); Harry Treadwell from *Cat World Weekly* (Pets); Lisa and Brian Stanley (Entertaining); Sandra Boler from *Brides* magazine (Weddings); Peter Beveridge (Money).

My special thanks to Judy Piatkus and Gill Cormode for conceiving the idea and having faith in me; Ursula Mackenzie for answering all my questions; Nick Welch for helping me realise in which direction this book should go; Mike and Paul for moral support, and Andrew for designing, reading, inspiring, listening and being supportive. Thanks also to Jack.

Introduction

How often do you make two telephone calls when one would do? How many times have you had to make a second journey to the shops for a forgotten ingredient? Are you the sort of person who loses vital telephone numbers, wrestles helplessly with broken equipment or runs out of wallpaper half way round the final wall? Do you long to be organised?

The Complete Book of Household Lists has been compiled for those who are already compulsive list-makers, and for those who are about to be initiated into this immensely satisfying way of life. The book contains over 200 different lists, covering every aspect of the home and household. They are practical, useful, inspirational and fun – and especially designed to make you organised too.

Lists are a minor art form, and they are also fairly sophisticated placebos. You feel that you have already broken the camel's back when you write out a list of your chores. You feel smug when you cross off items, particularly when you cross off those which shouldn't have been there anyway! You feel marvellously in control of your destiny when you see it there in black and white. Lists work because you can think them up in the peace and quiet of your home. You can then calmly and rationally place your chores in an appropriate order and plan your future. In only a few minutes you can save yourself hours of time-wasting confusion and worry.

I hope you enjoy using *Household Lists.* Use them to jog your memory. Adapt the lists to suit your particular needs. Follow them step by step and save yourself time – and money! Laugh at the fun lists, test yourself on the quiz lists and refer to them all time and time again. *The Complete Book of Household Lists* will inspire you to devise your own lists, and will help you to discover the simple satisfaction that comes from being organised.

Nina Grunfeld

Home

Can you afford to move?

Selling your home

Estate agent's fee*	£
Solicitor's fee*	£

Buying a home

Solicitor's fee (including acting for Building Society or other lender if you want a mortgage)*	£
Building Society or other lender's valuation fee (if you want a mortgage)	£
Your surveyor's fee*	£
Search fee	£
Land Registry fee	£
Stamp Duty, if relevant	£
Cost of necessary repairs, decorations, fittings, installations, etc	£
Cost of looking for home (time off work, petrol, fares, etc)	£

Other costs

Removal firm's charge*	£
Allowance for surveys, solicitor's fees, etc on deals which fall through	£
Interest on bridging loan from bank, if necessary	£
VAT on above costs, where relevant	£
Total	£

All these costs vary depending on how much you do yourself.

What do you really want?

General How much can you afford to spend, including moving, repairs, decorating, etc? See *Can you afford to move?* (page 14).

Would building an extension on your present home be an easier and cheaper solution to your space problems?

How much work are you prepared to do on any place you buy?

Do you want a home that's easy to look after?

Do you want a place that will be easy to sell? (On the whole, 'modern', three bedroom, semi-detached houses are easier to sell than houses 'with character'.)

Location What area do you want to live in?

Where is it important for you to be near? See *Where is your nearest...?* (page 20).

Do you want to be East/West or North/South facing?

Do you want a nice view?

Do you mind being on a main road?

How much privacy do you want?

Style Do you want a 'period' home?

If so, which periods are you interested in?

Do you want a detached/semi/terraced house or a flat or bungalow?

Is central heating important to you?

Do you want double glazing?

Size Do you want a home your family will be able to expand into?

How many rooms do you want?

How many bedrooms do you want?

How many bathrooms do you want?

Do you want a separate lavatory?

Do you want a separate dining room?

Do you want to be able to eat in the kitchen?

Do you have an enormous piece of furniture that has to be housed?

Do you want a garden? If so, would you like a large or small garden?

Do you want a garage? If so, for one, two or more cars?

Do you need any other outhouses?

Decide which points are your top priorities and which may be open to compromise. You will probably never find anywhere that is 100 per cent perfect—though you may be surprised!

Home in on...

The area – look for 'For Sale' signs.

Friends, relatives and work colleagues – they may know of houses for sale.

Newspapers, both national and local – check the property section and the personal columns.

Sunday papers.

Classified ads magazines.

Specialist magazines or newspapers aimed at home buyers.

Estate agents – first check that they belong to a professional body and then let them know that you're a serious buyer by telephoning them frequently to find out if any new buildings are on the market.

Auctions – find out about them in your local paper.

Estate agent's phrase book

Old-world charm:
Make sure you have a survey.

Ripe for conversion:
It's almost mouldy.

Original features:
Outside loo.

The decor is a trifle tired:
It's almost dropped off.

Mature garden:
If you can get into it.

Period style:
Mock something or other.

Architect designed home:
Aren't they all?

Imaginatively decorated:
No-one likes it.

Modernised to make optimum use of light and space:
It always will be dark, tiny and modern.

Easy to maintain:
There's only one room.

Fitted kitchen:
It's got cupboards.

Off-street parking:
On the pavement.

Occupying a bold corner site:
Traffic on both sides.

Ideally suited for town and country:
Suburbia.

---

3 minutes station:
Or jump on the train at the bottom of the garden.

Don't be fooled by...

Their excuse for selling. (What's the real reason?)

Their old survey. (Might it be somewhat out of date?)

The amount of property for sale in the street. (Does it imply an investment area or a future airport runway?)

The rows of locks on the front door. (Have you researched the area?)

The empty street. (Is it as easy to park at night?)

The charming pub next door. (Does it turn into a late night disco?)

The garage. (Is it wide enough for your car?)

The apparent quiet. (Have you just missed Concorde?)

The romantic seclusion of the house. (How self-sufficient are you?)

The friendly neighbours. (Do you like discussing your washing?)

The stunning garden. (Have you got green fingers?)

The attractive tree in the garden. (Is it causing the house to collapse?)

The picturesque river. (Does it ever flood?)

The neighbours' new roofs. (Will you also be needing one soon?)

The newly decorated basement. (Why did they need to do that?)

The enormous attic. (Is it insulated?)

The abundance of windows. (Will they all need double glazing?)

The original window frames. (Are they rotten?)

The charming lead plumbing. (When will it need replacing?)

The antique lamps. (Are they indicative of the state of the wiring?)

The large painting hanging where the fireplace used to be. (Is it concealing the absence of an air vent?)

The textured wallpaper. (What's it hiding?)

The unusual arch in the front room. (Was the wall load bearing?)

The sloping floor. (Is this a warning?)

The overwhelming smell of air freshener. (What might you have smelt otherwise?)

The charming fireplaces. (Have they never heard of central heating?)

The stunning balcony. (How often will you be able to use it?)

The sweet little staircase. (Will elders be able to manage?)

The number of bathrooms. (Is the hot water tank large enough for so many simultaneous baths?)

The sun streaming in through the windows. (Will it look the same when it's raining?)

The spacious rooms. (How much will it cost to heat them?)

The tiny front door. (Will your furniture get through?)

The cosy kitchen/dining room. (Will your family fit?)

The welcoming hall. (How will it look with your bicycle there?)

The lovely Persian carpets. (What are they hiding?)

The large number of little rooms. (Will it mean endless guests?)

The generous amount of fixtures and fittings they're leaving. (Do you want them?)

Their exquisite antique furniture. (Should you be buying that rather than their house?)

The abundant vases of flowers. (What will it look like without them?)

Their abysmal taste. (If that's the only thing that's wrong, you're lucky!)

Take with you...

A list of questions to find out the size of utility bills, what recent improvements have been made, etc.

Pencil and paper for note-taking.

A friend to distract the vendor so you can snoop.

Binoculars to study the view, the neighbours and the roof.

Heavy shoes to kick the skirting board to see if it crumbles, or to walk home in if there is no public transport.

Magnifying glass to look at cracks, woodworm and their old surveyor's report.

Compass to check you are facing the way they say.

A list of all the large pieces of furniture you own so that you can mentally try and fit them all in.

Tape measure to record room dimensions and to make quite sure your furniture will fit.

A list of the cupboard space you know you will need.

Perfume in case the smell of damp is too overpowering.

Camera for memory jogging.

Where is your nearest?

Underground station and/or bus stop
Main line railway station
Park
Playground
Doctor
Dentist
Hospital
Vet
Late night chemist
Local shop
Supermarket
Delicatessen
Shop open on a Sunday
Main shopping centre

Police station	Telephone booth
Bank	Launderette
Post office	Dry cleaner
Work	Sports centre
School(s)	Dance hall
Library	Good pub
Church	Good restaurant
Cinema	Take-away
Theatre	Garage mechanic
Bookshop	Petrol station

It is a nice idea to give anyone who moves into your neighbourhood a Where is your nearest? *list with all the addresses filled in. Maybe you should compile one for potential buyers when you decide to sell your home.*

Buying it

1. Start saving with a building society at least six months before you intend to buy.

2. If you need a mortgage, find out from your building society or bank how much they will lend you. They normally lend $2\frac{1}{2}$ times your annual salary.

3. Work out how much you can afford to spend. See *Can you afford to move?* (page 14).

4. Decide what you want. See *What do you really want?* (page 15).

5. Research the market.

6. Find the house you want to buy.

7. Ask to have a list of what fixtures and fittings are included in the price and what exactly the property consists of.

8. If the price of the property is just within a stamp duty category, try and apportion some of this to fixtures and fittings to bring the purchase price to below the limit and thus avoid paying stamp duty or paying a higher rate of stamp duty.

9. Make an offer subject to contract and survey.

10. When offer is accepted, estate agents will ask for a deposit in 'good faith'. Refuse to pay more than £100 and ensure that it is returned to you or taken off the purchase price on completion.

11. If you are not going to do your own conveyancing, find a solicitor.

12. Apply in writing for a mortgage and make sure you get one before going any further.

13. Arrange for a private survey of the property if you want one. Make sure that the surveyor is a member of a professional body.

14. Start the legal procedure.

15. Exchange contracts and pay a deposit of 10 per cent of the purchase price.

16. You are now committed to buying the house. Your solicitor will ensure that you or your building society insure the house the moment you exchange contracts.

17. If you are planning to hire a removal firm, get estimates or find out how best to do it yourself. See *Moving* section.

18. On completion date, pay the balance of the purchase price. This is normally paid by your building society. Move in.

The above list applies to buying a home in England and Wales; Scotland and Northern Ireland have a different house transfer system.

Note from a solicitor: *Never do your own conveyancing – you may think you understand, but you may not. If you make a mistake there is no redress against anyone. If a solicitor makes a mistake, you can sue him.*

Selling it

1. Look critically at your home and notice all its faults.

2. Carry out minor repairs both inside and out, such as filling in cracks, washing walls, fixing garden fence.

3. Don't over-invest as you may not recover your costs.

4. Find out what your home is worth.

5. Advertise it yourself.

6. Make a list of all the fixtures and fittings you want to sell.

7. Keep your home and garden clean and tidy until the deal is done.

8. Read *Don't be fooled by . . .* (page 18) and place vases of flowers and rugs strategically.

9. Keep your home well lit and warm in winter, and cool in summer.

10. Prepare 'facts' sheets for prospective buyers. Mention anything positive about your home, from planning permission obtained and never used to the proximity of shops and services.

11. If possible, avoid playing music when potential buyers visit in case they don't share your taste.

12. If you are not going to do your own conveyancing, find a solicitor.

13. Start the legal procedure.

14. If you don't think you have found a buyer after a month or so, appoint an established firm of estate agents.

15. When you receive an acceptable offer, accept it subject to contract.

16. Exchange contracts. Buyer pays 10 per cent of purchase price and is committed to buying your home. (You are also committed to selling it.)

17. Get estimates from removal firms.

18. Receive the balance of the purchase price on completion and move out.

The above list applies to selling a home in England and Wales; Scotland and Northern Ireland have a different house transfer system.

Moving

Moving yourself costs money

	Possible extras
You work out the cheapest van hire, but forget to include the cost of insurance . . . and VAT.	£
You calculate exactly how many miles you'll be travelling (for the 'x pence per mile' factor), but forget to cost in the extra trip with the contents of the garden shed . . . and the trip to return the van.	£
You are not used to driving such a large van, particularly one filled with everything you own, and you decide you need extra driving lessons.	£
You buy dozens of tea chests and plastic crates, but have to hire a van to get them home!	£
You need packing materials such as tape, string, mattress bags, wardrobe cartons and other useful things that professional removal firms have, but you don't.	£
All those able-bodied friends have offered to help, but you will have to buy food and drink and huge thank-you presents.	£
You don't know how to pick up your furniture correctly, and haven't allowed for osteopath's fees. (Always bend your knees when picking up and putting down heavy objects.)	£
You have a lot of heavy furniture and you have to hire a trolley on wheels to help shift it.	£
You forget to measure the width of your stairs and your furniture won't go up. Include the cost of a winch.	£

You are let down by your hired van driver (and van) – the last minute might be a rather expensive time to re-think your move!	£
You thought the van was big enough, and it is, but nothing can fit through its door. Allow extra costs for hiring a van with a tailboard.	£
You take so long loading that you need to hire the van for a second day!	£
You get bored (or broke) driving up and down the motorway and stopping at endless petrol stations to fill your bottomless tank. (Did you forget to ask how many miles the van does to the gallon?)	£
You have not quite mastered the art of van packing and your furniture slips, moves and breaks. Do you have adequate insurance?	£
Total	£

On the whole it's probably only a good idea to move yourself if you don't have many possessions and you don't have far to go.

Choosing a removal firm

Ask for quotations from at least three firms.

Show each of them your house, garden, garage and loft.

Point out any 'problems', such as tropical fish, garden statues, enormous deep-freeze.

Mention which furniture you are selling and which you are leaving behind.

Tell them what you will do and what you will pay them to do.

Unless otherwise agreed, most removers will:
1. Pack and unpack all china, glass, books and kitchen utensils.
2. Take apart (and re-assemble) bedsteads, wardrobes and other large pieces of furniture, apart from self-assembly furniture which you should dismantle before the move.
3. Take down (but not re-hang) wall-hangings, mirrors and pictures.
4. Take up (and re-lay) loose floor coverings, such as carpet squares and rugs. They may also lift your fitted carpets and linoleum (but they will not re-lay unless you ask).

Check their contract carefully.

Discuss insurance in detail. Ensure your goods will be covered during packing and unpacking, loading and unloading and while in transit.

Enquire whether there is extra insurance cover for electrical equipment and any articles of value.

Show them the plan of your new home and discuss any access problems.

Find out how many removal men there will be and how long each stage should take.

Find out if tea-chests and other packing cases will be supplied.

Discuss storage, if you need it.

Ask each removal firm to send you a quotation, stating what extra costs there might be.

Once you have decided which removal firm to use, choose with them the best day and time for the move.

Ask them to confirm in writing that they are fully insured against damage to your goods.

Send their letter and contract to your insurance broker for him to check.

Give the firm the go-ahead, if your insurance broker agrees, and start packing!

If possible use a removal firm that belongs to the British Association of Removers.

Moving countdown

1–4 weeks before **Decide** whether you want to move yourself with the help of friends, hire a van with a driver or hire the professionals. If you decide to use a professional removal firm, get quotations and book a firm well in advance. See *Choosing a removal firm* (page 26).

Beg, borrow or buy tea-chests or packing cases, even if you are using professionals.

Start packing as much as you can as soon as you can. See *Packing hints* (page 32).

Find out if the items you have packed are covered by removal firm's insurance.

Send the removal firm a written description or plan of where your new home is located. Give the firm the full address and telephone number (or number of a friend or new neighbour if the telephone is not connected).

Arrange for your new gas board to send a meter reader and fitter to your new home (if necessary on moving day itself), and for your old gas board to disconnect your gas supply.

Make sure your local electricity and water boards are given notice of your move. Arrange for meter readings, etc.

Try and arrange with your new telephone sales office for a new telephone to be installed, or to take over an existing line.

Arrange for your motor insurance to be changed, at least a week before you move.

Have your last pre-move washing session before unplumbing the washing machine.

Make arrangements for the appropriate electrician, plumber, fitter, etc to disconnect domestic appliances and reconnect them at your new address. Removers are not qualified to do this, and you probably are not either!

Search for manuals for stereo, video, tumble dryer, etc, and check moving instructions. Try and find old stereo boxes. Contact manufacturers if you have lost manuals.

Start running down freezer contents and de-frost. Give food to friends and neighbours to eat or store, if necessary. Note: expert opinion states that any movement of a freezer in a frozen condition involves risks to the cabinet, the mechanism and the food in it and you may find that removal firms will not accept responsibility for either the freezer or its contents.

Arrange for a carpet fitter to remove and re-lay floor coverings, including fitted carpets. Removal firms may spread out carpets in your new home but not re-lay them.

Take down curtains and blinds, and have them cleaned if they need it.

Dismantle any self-assembly furniture as joints are seldom strong enough to survive even careful handling when fully assembled.

Pack very small items (trinkets and valuables) yourself and seal them in a well-labelled box.

Stick 'Do Not Move' labels on any items which you have sold with the house.

Consider how to protect floors when moving and discuss with removers.

Move TV aerial, towel rails, pelmets and any other fixed items yourself.

Start decorating, fitting carpets and sanding floors in your new home, if possible.

Plan where you want to put the furniture.

Book hotel accommodation if you are going to need it either en route or for a day or two at the other end.

Throw a going-away party before you leave, and one for your children too.

0–7 days before **Check** garden sheds, corners of attic, cellar, etc, and bring out anything you or professional removers could overlook.

Lay out all china and glass for the removers to pack. Bear in mind that they will probably pack furniture into the van first.

Pack your load 'load last/unload first' box and make sure you mark it clearly. See *Load last/ unload first* (page 32).

Pack clothing and personal articles yourself or leave them for the removers to pack.

Dismantle garden shed(s) for loading, if they are going with you.

Clean and assemble garden tools and dustbins.

Drain fuel from paraffin heaters, motor mowers and oil lamps.

Remove batteries from portable gas-cooker lighters, etc.

Keep money, jewellery and documents with you at all times.

Make a detailed plan of your new home and decide in which room each packing case and piece of furniture should go. Label each case and piece of furniture with a code number, and mark it on the plan.

Warn the removers of any traffic restrictions outside either home, and arrange police co-operation.

Reserve a 15-metre (50-foot) parking space for the removal van if your road tends to get crowded.

Arrange for lifts to be vacant if you are moving in and/or out of a multi-storey block.

Strip beds, fold bedding and leave it stacked on the mattresses.

Leave drawers packed, unless very heavy, but don't lock them.

Keep hand-luggage with you. Don't let it get put in the van by mistake.

Arrange for children to be with friends or relations, or hire a babysitter for them and make sure they are kept well out of the way.

Assign older children specific tasks, so they become involved.

Keep pets out of the way in a safe place.

Pack plants securely in cardboard boxes, using foil at the bottom as a tray.

Show removers what has to be moved,

including items from garage, garden and attic.

Point out what is not to be moved (these items should have clear stickers on them).

Lay down protective coverings on any fitted carpets or delicate floors.

Give the removers the coded plan of your new home and make sure they understand it.

Make sure they have the exact address of your new home and a set of keys.

See that they know where to contact you if you are not going directly to your new address.

Tell them if there is anything you want first off the van at the destination. See *Load last/ unload first* (page 32).

Offer endless cups of tea (or coffee).

The final check

Yes/No

Is everything you want to take with you in your car or taxi?	
Have you left anything behind? (Take one last look around.)	
Are all water taps turned off?	
Is the main stopcock turned off as well?	
Is gas properly turned off at the meter?	
Have you turned off electricity at the mains?	
Are all windows shut and bolted or locked?	
Have you written your new address on a card and left it in the hall?	
Are the back, side and front doors locked?	
Have you surrendered house keys to new owner, estate agent or solicitor?	

Packing hints

Pack all articles carefully, making sure they cannot move around in their boxes.

Never rest anything heavy on top of fragile articles.

Pack groups of things together: all children's toys, all pots and pans, etc.

Mark each box with a list of what is inside, and make sure as few boxes as possible are labelled 'miscellaneous'.

Label each box with the code for the room it will go in in your new home.

Mark all boxes 'This Way Up'.

Make a complete inventory of all things packed, and keep it with you.

Pack all electrical appliances in their original boxes if possible.

Never fill tea-chests to the top with books – even removal men cannot lift them.

Load last/unload first

Lighting
Candles
Matches
Plugs
Screwdriver
Light bulbs
Torch

Cleaning
Dusters
Rags
Buckets
All-purpose cleaner
Disinfectant
Rubber gloves
Rubber sink plug
Tea towels
Scissors

Brush and pan
Vacuum cleaner

Personal
Soap
Towels
Washbag
    (toothbrush, etc)
Any medicaments
    you are taking
    regularly
Lavatory paper
Plasters
Coathangers
Curtains for
    bedroom(s) and
    bathroom

Extras

Pen and notepad
(make notes of
anything broken or
lost)
Toys for children
Coins for telephone
box
Radio (portable)

Food

Electric kettle (or
camping stove and
saucepan if no
electricity)
Can opener
Tea, coffee, sugar
and powdered or
canned milk
Bread and biscuits
Bottle of wine (screw-
topped) or
champagne
Paper cups and
plates
Knives and spoons
Pet food

Just moved - who to tell

The new occupants
of your old home
Friends and relatives
Local gas board
Local electricity
board
Water board
Town Hall (rates) etc
Local telephone
sales office
Post Office
Personal Giro
Premium bonds
Save as You Earn
and National
Saving Certificates
Inland Revenue
National Savings
Bank
Your bank(s)
Credit card(s)
HP companies
All insurance
companies,
including BUPA
Other professional
advisors: solicitor,
accountant,
stockbroker, etc
Doctor
Dentist
Optician
Vet
Hospital/clinic
National Insurance
DHSS benefits/
allowances
Pension book
Vehicle Registration
Document
Driving Licence
Residents Parking
Permit
TV Broadcast
Receiving Licence
TV rental firm
Publications you
subscribe to
Mail Order
companies
Local business
accounts
Football pools
Children's school(s)
Library
Your employer
Your landlord/
tenants
Any organisations
and clubs you
belong to

Decorating

Designing your home

General Collect pictures of rooms you like and work out why they appeal to you.

Never slavishly follow magazine design ideas unless you are sure they suit your home, your lifestyle and your finances.

Decorate to impress yourself and not your friends.

Design your home to suit your lifestyle. (Don't choose pale and delicate fabrics and place bijou art objects everywhere if you have boisterous children or dogs.)

Make sure your home doesn't look too fashionable. (It may appear dated tomorrow.)

Try to complement the style of your building rather than ignore it.

Colour Use one floor colour throughout the house to give a unified look and make your home appear larger.

Try and relate the colour scheme of one room to that of another.

For simple success, stick to one of four colour schemes: monochromatic (shades of one colour); related (similar colours such as reds and oranges); contrasting (opposite colours, such as orange and turquoise); or primary (primary colours, several or just one, with white).

Beware of using more than one basic colour scheme, a couple of subsidiary colours and two patterns in one room.

If you are nervous of using colour and pattern, choose bright colours or patterns for cushions, rugs, paintings, etc, and keep everything else monochromatic.

Play tricks with colours. Use light colours to make walls recede, dark colours to make rooms seem more compact.

Never rush into painting a naturally dark room white in an attempt to brighten it; dark rooms can be most effective and very cosy.

Blend awkward pipes and radiators into the background by painting them the same colour as the walls, or paint them a contrasting colour and turn them into a feature.

Texture Choose textures you like. If you wear a lot of silk, use soft shiny fabrics in your home and if you are happy in tweeds, select natural weave fabrics.

Use the right materials and colours in the right rooms. (Never put dark, sophisticated curtains in the laundry room or an expensive carpet in the nursery.)

Try experimenting with different textures of fabrics.

Use loose covers; not only is furniture protected, but you can change the atmosphere of a room in minutes. Use loose covers in summer over heavy covered winter chairs.

Hints Throw out things you don't really like (including presents, if you can do it tactfully); a compromise never works.

Buy the best furniture you can afford, or use obvious temporary measures, such as orange boxes for tables and the garden swing as a sofa!

Keep rooms as empty as possible, or jam-packed with your collections of fans, kites or Victorian glass.

Fill rooms with your creations. Paint pictures, frame your tapestries or cultivate masses of plants.

Use mirrors everywhere, for light, space and illusion.

Be imaginative with lighting. Use lights to create different atmospheres.

Enjoy pictures. Use one enormous painting as a focal point or lots of prints in a row along a wall.

Treat yourself to cushions, not only for comfort but for a luxurious look too.

Don't be afraid to mix modern and antique furniture.

Make sure you can afford the Persian carpet etc, before you plan your room around it.

Before choosing colours, look at them in both daylight and artificial light. See *Painting hints* (page 44).

Take samples of existing carpets, curtains, etc with you when shopping, to match them.

Before calling in the decorator, make sure both you and your partner agree on all design schemes. If that is impossible, take a few rooms each and do what you want with them.

Before you decorate...

Do all structural work, major alterations and improvements before you start decorating.

Add extensions or loft conversions if you can afford to, or even if you think you can't, and avoid total chaos a second time.

Knock down non-load-bearing walls to make larger rooms.

Fill in walls others have knocked down and make smaller, cosier rooms.

Put in a damp-proof course.

Deal with any dry or wet rot, leaking roofs and gutters, woodworm, etc.

Replace windows. Think about double glazing.

Check electric wiring and rewire.

Move electric power points and lights to where you will want them and add plenty of new ones – you can never have enough.

Install central heating or make sure existing radiators are in the most suitable place and that there are enough.

Open up fireplaces and alcoves. Make the most of any original features.

Insulate the loft, wall cavities, etc.

Check plumbing and kitchen and bathroom fittings.

Renew plasterwork.

Sand floors, doors, bannisters and skirting boards.

If you are living 'on site', try to complete one room at a time and then move into it until the entire house is finished. Start with the kitchen, bathroom and a room to sleep in.

If you've been lucky enough to move into a place that only needs a coat of paint or, if you've now reached that stage, read on.

Preparation work

General preparation

Remove or cover all furniture.

Take down curtains, lampshades and anything screwed to the wall.

Cover the floor with dustsheets or newspapers.

Remove the carpet if you are worried about it.

Dust or vacuum all surfaces.

Preparation for wallpapering

Newly plastered walls: Paint first with a coat of sizing to provide a non-porous surface for paste.

Plasterboard: Treat any nailheads with rust inhibitive primer, then apply a coat of sealer.

Old wallpaper (porous): Brush on warm water, leave to soak then scrape off with a stripping knife. Re-soak stubborn patches. Finish by washing walls with clean water to remove last scraps of paper and paste. It is advisable to remove old wallpaper rather than papering over it, even if it is in a good condition.

Washable (or gloss-painted) wallpapers: Scratch with steel wire brush to allow water or stripping solution to penetrate surface, then scrape off and wash as old wallpaper above.

Vinyl wallpaper: Lift the bottom corners and peel the entire length of plastic surface away from its backing which should remain stuck to the wall. Leave paper backing for re-papering (or painting) on. If paper tears, strip away backing paper as well.

Painted surfaces: Wash with warm soapy water, rinse and dry, then sandpaper lightly before pasting.

Old distemper: Wash off and apply a coat of stabilising primer.

Damp walls: Treat mould growth with fungicide. Rub efflorescence (white, powdery deposit) down with coarse hessian and paint with an alkali-resistant primer. Never paper over damp walls.

Cracked walls: Dig loose plaster out of holes and cracks and fill with cellulose thinner. Rub down with sandpaper when dry.

Preparation for wall painting

New plaster, concrete or brick: Allow roughly three months for walls to dry out. Rub off efflorescence and paint area with an alkali-resistant primer. Give porous or rough-textured surfaces an initial coat of thinner paint and leave for 12 hours before painting as normal.

Old brick or concrete: Scrub with detergent solution, then apply a coat of stabilising primer before painting.

Plasterboard: Treat nailheads with rust inhibitive primer, then paint. Several coats of paint may be needed.

Wallpaper (good condition): Brush clean and remove any grease marks with blotting paper and a hot iron.

Wallpaper (bad condition): Strip off (see *Preparation for wallpapering*, above) and re-line the wall.

Painted surfaces (good condition): Wash with detergent solution, rinse and dry thoroughly before painting. If painted with gloss or eggshell, sand with fine sandpaper to ensure paint sticks to surface.

Flaking paintwork: Remove flaking paint with a stripping knife and sand edges of damaged areas gently. If the flaking is extensive, apply a coat of stabilising primer.

Damp walls: First treat the problem and let the area dry thoroughly before applying a multi-purpose primer. Treat any mould growth with mild (1 : 16) bleach solution, leave for four hours and repeat. Paint wall properly after three days.

Cracked walls: Treat as for wallpapering. If cracks are large it may be necessary to use lining paper before painting.

Preparation for woodwork painting

New woodwork: Sand surface gently to smooth. Paint any knots with shellac coating to stop resin coming through to finished paintwork. Use primer to reveal irregularities in wood. Fill all dents, scratches, etc with fine grain or wood filler and sand when dry. Paint on two coats of undercoat and then one of gloss, leaving paint to dry between each coat.

Old paintwork (good condition): Wash with water and sugar soap, rinse and dry thoroughly. Gently rub area with fine sandpaper first, then apply undercoat.

Old paintwork (bad condition): Wash and dry as above, then either burn off old paint with a blowlamp (use with care) or, if you want a natural sealed wood finish, use a chemical paint stripper. After stripping, treat wood as new woodwork above.

Preparation for tiling

Brick and concrete: Scrub the surface with a brush to remove all loose material. If the surface is uneven, you may have to screed the wall.

New plaster or plasterboard: Once the surface is dry, coat it with a multi-purpose primer to make sure it doesn't absorb any moisture from the tile adhesive.

Old plaster: Dig any loose plaster out of holes and cracks and fill them with cellulose thinner. Rub down with sandpaper when dry.

Painted surfaces (good condition): Wash with detergent solution and when dry scratch with sandpaper.

Painted surfaces (bad condition): Remove flaking paint with a stripping knife and apply a coat of stabilising primer.

Wallpaper: Never tile over wallpaper. Strip off paper and prepare wall as for new plaster above.

Old tiles: Clean with detergent solution and repair any cracks or loose tiles.

Finish all preparation work before you start decorating.

When decorating a room, always paint the ceiling first, then walls and then the woodwork. If the walls and/or ceiling are to be papered, do these last. The paintwork must be completely dry before you start to paper.

Tools of the trade

Preparation
Sanding block and various types of abrasive paper for sanding down rough woodwork and excess plaster.

Stripping knife for stripping off old wallpaper and smoothing plaster.

Chisel knife for removing old paint and small areas of plaster.

Bolster for hacking away at loose or cracked plaster.

Shave-hook for preparing mouldings and crevices.

Blowlamp for burning off old paint.

Soft bristled brush or old paintbrush for dusting.

Steel wire brush for scratching wallpaper.

Putty knife for replacing window panes.

Hawk or use a piece of hardboard or thick card, for applying small amounts of plaster.

Metal float for smoothing down large areas of plaster.

Overalls

Wallpapering   **Wallpapering scissors**

Trimming knife for cutting paper round fixtures, fittings and other protrusions.

Steep tape/wood rule for accurate measuring.

Plumb bob or use fine string with a weight attached, to help hang paper straight.

Seam roller to ensure seams stay stuck down, not to be used with embossed paper.

Paper hanging brush for smoothing on paper.

Pasting brush or large paint brush, but ensure good quality so that the bristles don't shed.

Bucket with string tied across the top against which to wipe off excess paste.

Water trough if using ready-pasted wallpapers.

Pencil

Folding table or kitchen table, for pasting wallpaper on.

Stepladder or two for papering ceiling, stairwell, etc.

Board/plank for using across the two stepladders for ceiling, stairwell, etc.

Dustsheets

Painting   **75mm (3″) painting brush**

50mm (2″) painting brush

25mm (1″) painting brush

Roller and tray with three roller covers: mohair for gloss paint, lambswool or nylon for emulsion paint and lambswool for textured surfaces.

Paint pads are often used instead of brushes.

Radiator brush

Cutting-in brush or cut off an old brush at a 45-degree angle, for painting window frames.

Razor blade scraper for removing paint from window panes when dry.

Paint shield for painting windows, or use masking tape but remember to pull tape off the moment paint is dry.

Petroleum jelly to rub on hands before painting to make them easier to clean.

Newspaper and rags to help clean brushes.

Empty glass jars for putting brushes in to clean.

Bath hat to wear when painting ceilings.

Dustsheets

Tile laying **Scriber** with a tungsten carbide tip for scoring and cutting tiles.

Tile nippers/pincers for nipping bits off tiles.

Adhesive spreader/trowel notched to ensure even spreading of adhesive.

Spreader for applying grout to tiled area.

Sponge for cleaning off excess grout.

Spirit level to ensure straight surface.

Pencil

How much paint?

Type of paint	500ml can	1 litre can	2½ litres can	5 litres can
Gloss and eggshell	6–7	12–14	30–35	60–70
Undercoat	5–6	11	28	55
Vinyl matt and vinyl silk	6–8	11–15	28–38	55–75
Weatherproof	–	–	12–25	25–50

Figures show the number of square metres covered by one can of paint. To convert these figures to square feet, multiply them by 10.

Painting hints

Never trust a tiny colour chart for choosing colours as they always appear lighter on the chart. Buy the smallest tin of paint and try it out.

Always buy enough paint to avoid a possible colour difference between batches. See *How much paint?* (page 43).

Use the right paint for the job, and don't skimp on paint or equipment.

Read *Preparation work* (page 38) and *Tools of the trade* (page 41).

Always follow manufacturer's instructions.

Before you stir paint, remove any skin that has formed. If skin has already been stirred in, strain paint through fine muslin or mesh.

Never paint straight from the tin. Put paint in a 'paint kettle' (an old can with a handle) and put the lid back on the paint pot to keep remaining paint clean.

Never dip more than one-third of your brush into the paint.

Always brush out each application before adding another.

Work away from any natural light, so that you can see what you are doing.

Paint edges and corners of walls/ceilings with a brush first and then paint the middle with a roller.

Paint walls without a break to avoid 'stop and start' edges, especially with gloss paint. Only stop when you reach a corner.

When painting a ceiling, work with your back to the light. Begin at the corner nearest the window and paint in bands parallel to the window across the room.

To paint your ceiling without a stepladder, fit a long handle to your roller.

If painting a ceiling, wear a shower cap or put a sheet of cardboard or a paper plate over the handle of your brush to catch the drips.

Always leave paint to dry thoroughly before applying the next coat.

Keep checking paint after you've applied it; you may be able to brush out any runs while paint is still wet.

Gloss paint should have two undercoats and a top coat and be sanded down in between each one.

Never brush out gloss paint too thinly, and always finish painting with light upward strokes.

If gloss paintwork looks patchy when dry, apply a second, or even a third, coat.

Avoid wearing woollen clothing when using gloss paint as any loose fibres may ruin the finish.

When painting windows, paint about 3mm ($\frac{1}{8}$ inch) over window panes to stop rain seeping in behind putty.

Shield carpet with sticky tape when painting skirting board, or use a stiff sheet of card to hold the carpet back.

Remember to clean out keyholes before painting doors, or dirt will be picked up by the brush.

If you can't complete gloss work in a day, wash brushes and keep them in white spirit overnight.

Try to paint external woodwork or walls at the end of summer when they should be dried out. Never paint just after (or before) a rainfall.

Finish outside gloss painting at least two hours before sunset, or dew might spoil the finish.

Clean equipment thoroughly after use.

Hammer tops on paint tins and then tip tin over to form an airtight seal.

Store gloss paint with a layer of white spirit on the top to stop a skin forming.

After use, store brushes horizontally or hang them up.

Fill a small bottle with the paint you've used and keep for touch-ups. Remember to mark which room it's for.

How much wallpaper?

Walls   Measure the height of your room from the skirting board up, and then measure the perimeter of your room, including doors and windows.

Figures show the number of rolls of wallpaper required.

Distance around the room	Height from skirting			
	2.2m (7'6")	2.5m (8'6")	2.8m (9'6")	3.1m (10'6")
10m (32')	4	5	5	5
12m (40')	5	6	6	7
15m (48')	6	7	7	8
17m (56')	7	8	9	10
19m (64')	8	9	10	11
22m (74')	9	10	11	12
24m (80')	11	13	14	16

Ceilings   To work out the number of rolls required, calculate the area in square metres and divide by 5.

Remember, you may have to allow for more paper if you use a repeating pattern with a large repeat.

The wallpaper code

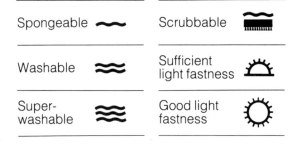

Spongeable	〰	Scrubbable	🟫
Washable	≈	Sufficient light fastness	☼
Super-washable	≋	Good light fastness	☀

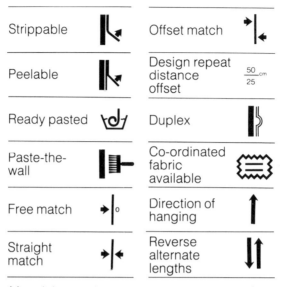

Strippable		Offset match	
Peelable		Design repeat distance offset	$\frac{50}{25}$ cm
Ready pasted		Duplex	
Paste-the-wall		Co-ordinated fabric available	
Free match		Direction of hanging	
Straight match		Reverse alternate lengths	

Material reproduced with the permission of the Wallpaper Marketing Board.

Wallpapering hints

Buy all the wallpaper you need at the same time. See *How much wallpaper?* (page 46).

Remember, the larger the pattern repeat, the more wallpaper you'll need.

Make sure all the rolls you buy carry the same batch number.

Check that all the rolls are the same colour; use any slightly different shades in alcoves, on window walls or in corners.

Always store wallpaper flat. Never stand rolls on end or you will damage the edges.

Read *Preparation work* (page 38) and *Tools of the trade* (page 41).

Always follow any manufacturer's instructions, both for paper and paste.

Check whether you need lining paper on your walls and ceiling. It may only be necessary if walls are in poor condition: wallpaper is very expensive or you wish to paint walls afterwards.

Only buy good quality lining paper and hang it with the adhesive recommended for the final wallcovering.

Always hang lining paper horizontally (in the opposite direction to the wallpaper) and never overlap joins.

Allow lining paper to dry for at least 24 hours before papering final layer or painting.

Try to remove radiators before papering. If impossible, use a wire coat-hanger taped to a wooden handle and covered with cloth in order to ease the paper down behind the radiator.

If possible, remove electric plates or switches from walls, then paper behind them and replace, rather than papering and trimming. (Remember to turn off electricity at mains before unscrewing any electrical outlet.)

If your paper is plain or has a small pattern, start papering near a corner on the window wall and work round the room to the door in both directions.

If paper has a large pattern, centre it in a prominent place, such as above the fireplace, and work outwards in both directions.

Hang all ceiling paper parallel to the main window in the room, starting at the window and working away from it.

Cut wallpaper, especially large patterns, so that the main pattern unit appears at the top of the wall after trimming.

If matching patterns, work from two or three rolls at the same time to reduce wastage.

Cut several lengths of paper at once, always checking that the design matches before cutting.

Number lengths on the back so that you know in which order to hang them, and also which way up to hang them.

On each length allow an extra 50mm (2

inches) top and bottom for positioning and trimming.

Always glue from the centre of the paper out to the edges. Avoid letting the glue seep underneath the paper onto the right side.

Make sure each length is evenly soaked with glue and for the same amount of time.

Carry paper so that there is a large fold at the top and a smaller one at the bottom, with pasted surfaces together.

When you reach the wall, hold the top end by the corners and let the paper unfold.

To hang the first strip of paper accurately, use a plumb bob.

When paper is in place, brush it out from the centre, smoothing out any creases or air bubbles.

If using very long lengths of paper, for example in a stairwell, ask someone to hold the paper so that it doesn't tear.

If wrinkles appear when sticking the paper to the wall, gently peel paper back then brush it down again. Minor wrinkles may disappear on drying.

To remove difficult air bubbles, use a knife with a sharp point and prick them, then brush the paper out flat.

If a bit of paper refuses to stay flat, push extra paste under it and press hard.

Always have a sponge or cloth handy to wipe off excess paste.

Never hang a length of paper so that more than 10mm ($\frac{1}{2}$ inch) goes round to the adjoining wall. Cut it before hanging and brush it well into the corner.

Always establish another vertical with your plumb bob once you turn a corner.

Questions and answers

1. How do you get mould off paintwork, in particular off window frames?
Mould is usually associated with condensation on frames. Treat paintwork with a fungicidal wash to kill off spores. Unfortunately, bleach has no lasting effect.

2. Can you deaden the noise of a hi-fi coming through a shared wall?
No, once noise gets into the fabric of the house there's little you can do. Ask your neighbours to re-site the hi-fi!

3. Is it possible to tile over old tiles?
Yes, if they are clean and firm you can stick modern thin ceramic tiles over the top.

4. Is there a simple way of removing layers of old wallpaper?
Hire a steam wallpaper stripper. The steam will loosen the paper right through to the wall, and you will get it off by the piece.

5. How can one level an uneven concrete floor?
Use what is called a screeding compound. It usually involves mixing a powder with water and spreading it over the floor. No great skill is involved.

6. After the party a wet glass caused white ring marks to be left on a table. Is it possible to remove the rings?
Try cigar ash damped with water and rubbed over the rings. If this fails, try metal polish wadding or a light smear of cellulose thinners. Then re-wax.

7. Cracks in wall plaster keep re-appearing. Is there anything stronger than cellulose filler?
There is, but it probably won't hold either. The problem may be slight movement of the foundations as the soil expands and contracts. Unfortunately, no filler can withstand such movement.

8. How does one insulate awkward-to-get-at spots in a loft?

Either push glass fibre blanket into the spaces with a rake or broom, or use sheet expanded polystyrene pushed into place. Where impossible to reach, insulate the underside of the ceiling.

9. How can you tell by appearance who owns a fence?

You can't. Often the good side of your fence faces your neighbour, but there is no hard and fast rule. Consult the plans.

10. How can you seal off a stain which keeps bleeding through emulsion on a ceiling?

Clean the ceiling and apply a coat of aluminium primer sealer to the stained area. Allow to dry, and re-decorate.

List of ten most frequently asked questions on DIY kindly compiled by Do It Yourself *magazine.*

Shopping

Clever shopping

Always make a list of what you want to buy and double-check it.

Always research prices and quality before you buy.

Always shop alone, unless for a major household item.

Never shop with rich friends, or your children.

Always leave your credit cards at home.

Never take more money with you than you want to spend.

Always check the cash register and receipts.

Always take with you a tape measure and list of relevant measurements if buying things for the home.

Always take the actual item or a colour swatch with you if you want to match colours.

Always dress up when going clothes shopping or you may be intimidated by elegant assistants and buy more than you need.

Never go shopping for food on an empty stomach.

Always avoid shopping at local shops which will be more expensive, but never drive twenty miles for a small saving.

Never spurn a shop's 'own brands', they're usually at least 10 per cent cheaper than branded goods.

Always compare food costs in terms of cost per unit of weight, measure or serving rather than per pack or tin (take a calculator!).

Always check the bottom shelves in supermarkets in case those goods have not been marked up.

Never buy fresh or frozen foods in bulk if you won't get round to eating it all, but always consider buying non-perishables in bulk.

Always take advantage of special offers and seasonal bargains if you can. (You can always

deep freeze surplus food or share costs with
friends.)

Never pay the asking price for houses or
antiques.

Always haggle if you can, particularly at
street markets.

Never buy daytime clothes in artificial light.

Never buy clothes a size too small and say
you're going to slim.

Buying an appliance

How much do you want to spend?

Have you shopped around to see what is
available?

What particular job do you need it for?

Have you done your market research? See
Market research (page 55).

How much will it cost to run?

Do you mind if it's not the latest model? (You
might be able to find an earlier model at a
cheaper price.)

Will the shop deliver?

Have you got space in your home?

Will you need extra wiring or plumbing, and
will it be possible to put it where you want it?

Will the shop arrange for the complete
installation and assembly of the machine? If
not, can they recommend anyone?

Is there a service and instruction manual
available?

Will the appliance be easy to look after?

Can you get a maintenance contract if you
want one and can it be renewed?

How much will the minimum charge be for a
future service call?

Have you read the guarantee? See *How to
check a guarantee* (page 56).

Market research

	Yes/No
Have you asked friends who already have what you are thinking of buying?	
Have you read advertisements and manufacturers' leaflets, which are biased but do contain factual information?	
Have you read newspaper and magazine articles?	
Have you listened to radio and television programmes, if you can find a relevant one?	
Have you looked at useful copies of *Which?* magazine, published by The Consumers' Association?	
Have you consulted your local Consumer Advice Centre?	
Have you been given a demonstration?	
Have you checked labels on products, such as British Standards Institution Kitemark, BEAB (British Electro-Technical Approvals Board) mark of safety, Design Centre, British Gas, etc?	
Have you looked out for the relevant trade association symbol displayed in shops? It implies improvement of traders' standards of service to customers, but gives no extra legal rights?	
Have you found out if the retailer has got a good reputation?	

If you answered 'Yes' to at least 75 per cent of the above questions, you have probably done sufficient market research.

How to check a guarantee

Check whether the shop or the manufacturer is guaranteeing the purchase.

Check that they have a good reputation.

Check the length of the guarantee.

Check whether it covers the entire product or only certain parts.

Check what potential failures are excluded from the guarantee.

Check if it includes the cost of labour or only replacement parts.

Check if VAT on parts and labour is covered by the guarantee.

Check that the nominal 'visit' charge is under guarantee too.

Check whether you have to return the product to the shop or pay postage or transport charges to the factory?

Check whether you will be supplied with substitute goods while your product is being repaired.

Check what level of servicing or repair you will have to maintain to keep the guarantee valid.

Check what will happen if the shop closes down.

Check what will happen if you move.

Do check guarantees carefully; they can mean the difference between buying one product or another.

When you've bought it

Paperwork   Make sure you are given a dated receipt, and file it away when you get home.

If necessary, send back the special guarantee card.

File away any guarantee card that came with the product, and write the purchase date on it.

Keep any advertisement you may have seen about your product that makes any claims and/or guarantees about its performance.

Every now and again, check the performance of your product against any claims made on an advertisement. You have a right to complain if your product does not live up to them.

Installation   Read and follow any instructions very carefully. If there are no instructions with the product don't touch anything – write away for instructions and wait until they arrive.

See that the product is correctly installed. If you can't install it yourself, get it done professionally or ask the shop to help.

Keep packing boxes for at least two weeks, or for the period specified during which you may return goods if not satisfied. (Keep packing boxes for stereos and other fragile products indefinitely for a future move.)

Faults   If you can return a faulty product within two weeks, do use it as often as possible during that time to test for imperfections.

If anything goes wrong, stop using it immediately and check the guarantee.

Never attempt a do-it-yourself repair on an item under guarantee as it may invalidate the guarantee.

Keep a written record of dates on which you had the product serviced and keep all service receipts with the problem clearly stated on them. If the guarantee period ends and the problem starts again, you will be able to establish that the problem started while the product was under guarantee.

Always make a note of the name of the person you dealt with. Apart from being polite, talking to the same person helps you keep a closer check on what is going on.

Buying by post

Always check that the magazine, catalogue or newspaper containing the advertisement is up to date before you order.

Never rely solely on a photograph or illustration. Read the description giving dimensions, weight, etc.

Never buy if there is any important information missing.

Always try and find out everything you can about the reputation of the company you are about to deal with.

Always look into the conditions of sale and/or guarantees. Find out what happens if you are dissatisfied with the product.

Always be explicit in your instructions. Fill in all the information required, and don't forget to give your name and full postal address.

Always keep a copy of your order and a note of the date it was sent.

Always note in your diary the approximate date you expect goods to arrive, so that you can start chasing the company if they don't.

Always keep details of the advertisement, when it appeared, the advertiser's address and the main points (or make a photocopy).

Never send cash through the post.

Always send cheques or postal orders if you're asked to pay in advance.

Always ensure that you fill in cheque stubs or counterfoils.

Always order at least 3–4 weeks before you want the goods to arrive, especially during the Christmas rush.

Always inspect the product the moment you receive it, to make sure nothing is broken or missing and that you've been sent the correct item or the correct size.

Always return the product promptly and by recorded delivery.

Always send a letter stating what is wrong. Include your name, address, account number, date of order, description and cost of product.

Always ask for a full refund.

Always keep a duplicate copy of your correspondence with the company.

cleaning

Ideal cleaning gear

Vacuum cleaner plus attachments.

Carpet brush if vacuum can't reach corners.

Carpet sweeper but not necessary if you have a vacuum.

Yellow cotton dusters one for every room.

Sponge cloths one for bathroom and one for kitchen.

Paper towels if you can afford them.

Old sheets, shirts, etc make marvellous wraps.

Fake or real chamois cloths for cars and windows.

Long-handled soft broom so you don't ruin your back.

Squeezy sponge floor mop with replaceable head.

Scrubbing brush for keen cleaners.

Lavatory brush and stand.

Old toothbrushes for cleaning behind taps and in cracks.

Bottle brush.

Washing-up brush or twin action scouring and cleaning pads.

Steel wool pads which can be cut in half to make them last longer.

Plastic washing-up bowl the right shape to fit in your sink.

Dish cloths.

Plastic bucket(s).

Rubber gloves and hand cream.

Hearth and flue brushes for those with fires.

Yard broom if you need to sweep outside.

Feather duster fun for shelves you can't usually reach.

Cleaning

Useful cleaning products

Washing-up liquid
Household soap (bar or flakes)
Washing powder
Enzyme detergent (for soaking burnt saucepans)
Scouring powder
Liquid non-abrasive scouring cream
Disinfectant
Household bleach
Household ammonia (use with care)
Washing soda (for paintwork)
Bicarbonate of soda (for insides of fridges)
Methylated spirit (for silver and windows)
Oven cleaner
Liquid bath cleaner
Vinegar (for chrome taps)
Ketchup or brown sauce (for bronze or copper)
Floor and wall cleaner
Floor polish
Furniture polish
Carpet cleaner
Upholstery shampoo
Window-cleaning preparation
Metal polish
Silver polish

Remember to keep cleaners locked up and away from children.

Always read instructions.

See Stain removal kit *(page 191).*

Clean now - relax later

Put things away once you've used them, and get everyone else to do the same. (Saves massive tidying-up time later.)

Clean up spills immediately. (Saves elbow-grease later.)

Straighten crooked pictures.

Tidy up as often as possible; an orderly place looks cleaner.

Empty all waste paper baskets and dustbins daily.

Throw away dead flowers.

Empty ashtrays after use.

Plump cushions after squashing.

Vacuum the most used bits of living room and dining room carpets daily – it also helps preserve them.

Use throw-away paper napkins, tablecloths, etc. (Saves ironing time.)

Throw away anything you find you haven't used in the past year. (Saves tidying away time.) See *How to get rid of it* (page 68).

Don't leave clothes lying around, either air them or put them away. (Saves ironing time, and your clothes.)

Air your bed during breakfast and make it immediately afterwards.

Put dirty laundry in a box, basket or bag, don't leave it lying around.

Replace lavatory paper rolls, fold and hang up bathroom towels.

Wipe bath immediately after use, or use bubble bath and be lazy.

Clean the lavatory daily.

Sweep or vacuum bathroom and kitchen floors every few days.

Place a lid or net over frying pan, or cover surrounding area with newspaper. (Saves scrubbing floors time.)

Roast joints in aluminium foil, unwrapping them for the last 15 minutes to brown. (Saves cleaning oven time.)

Wipe over cooker and worktops after use. (Saves stain removal time.)

Line kitchen shelves and drawers with wipe-clean paper, and replace when dirty.

Wash pots, pans and cooking utensils as you cook, and use non-stick pans.

Wash dishes the moment you've used them, or soak them.

Leave everything to drain and dry, except silver, glasses and cutlery.

Swill sinks with water after use. (Saves scrubbing the tide marks later.)

Clean out and re-lay the fire first thing in the morning. (Saves doing it when you need a fire.)

Weekly or fortnightly...

Clean the bathroom and lavatory thoroughly, using lots of disinfectant.

Clean the kitchen, including the fridge, oven, bins, larder and all horizontal surfaces.

Clean the drain by pouring boiling water and a handful of washing soda down the kitchen sink.

Clean the rest of your home by dusting first then vacuuming. Remember to dust a room from top to bottom.

Polish furniture. Never polish a damp surface and always put the polish on the cloth and not directly onto the furniture.

Clean any hard floors. Have them sealed so you don't have to polish them.

Clean all mirrors.

Clean one room thoroughly. Do a different room once a fortnight, and once you've done the whole place take a fortnight off.

Visit the dry cleaner if necessary, and do your mending and ironing.

Clean up your finances – do all the household clerical and accounting work.

'Spring' cleaning

Clean out dreaded areas: under stairs, tops of cupboards, cellars.

Move heavy wardrobes and other large pieces and dust behind them.

Go through all drawers, desks and cupboards and throw away everything you don't want or use.

Dust all books and bookcases.

Wash paintwork, and don't forget to wash above door architraves, cupboards, etc.

Wash washable walls. Start at the bottom and work up or dirty water will run down and streak the bottom half of the wall.

Wash washable ceilings, including light fittings.

Wash or dry clean curtains, loose covers and cushion covers. Remember to hang substitute curtains, especially in the bedroom.

Clean windows or, if remotely dangerous, call in a window cleaner.

Sweep any used chimneys.

Shampoo carpets and upholstery.

Air and turn mattresses according to manufacturer's instructions.

Wash or dry clean all blankets and bedcovers.

Clean out kitchen cupboards and throw away anything that looks old.

Wipe down all spice jars and glass bottles that are on display.

De-frost the freezer. Upright freezers should be defrosted every three months, chest freezers every six months.

Polish whatever silver and copper you have.

Depending on your energy, 'Spring' cleaning can take place once a year or once every three months. That decision is yours.

Maintenance

Your tool box

450g (16oz) claw hammer to be held near the base for maximum effect.

Small pin hammer.

Electrician's screwdriver with insulated shaft.

Medium and small screwdrivers for general use, but not for opening cans of paint.

Crosshead screwdriver.

Bradawl for starting off screws and nails.

Tenon saw.

Junior hacksaw for cutting almost anything light.

Set of flat-sided chisels.

50mm (2 inch) bolster chisel for lifting up floorboards.

Pliers with wire cutters at the side.

Combination oilstone for sharpening chisels or take them to your local DIY shop.

Plane for making sticky doors fit.

Spirit level for both vertical and horizontal surfaces.

Steel tape measure with both imperial and metric measurements.

Hand drill with bits or an electric one.

Trimming knife.

G clamp to hold wood together while gluing it.

Try square for cutting wood square. Buy one with a 45-degree angle too.

Nail punch to hit nails below the surface.

Adjustable spanner and small spanners.

Sandpaper or sandblock.

Oil can.

Always buy the best quality tools you can afford, but hire them if you are only going to use them once.

*Always rub tools after use with an oily rag (use
sewing machine oil as it contains paraffin) to
clean them.*

Never throw away...

Light bulbs (unless
  broken)
Fuses (3 and 13
  amp)
Fuse wire
Square pin plugs
Spare adapters
Candles
Dynamo torch
Insulating tape
Spare 3-core flex
String
Elastic bands
Sellotape
Masking tape
Any adhesive
Safety pins
Paper clips
Drawing pins
Assorted nails,
screws, etc
Picture hooks
Curtain hooks
Empty jam jars
Large dustbin bags
Old plastic shopping
  bags
Plastic sheeting
Aluminium foil
Dust sheets
Old newspapers
Rags
Foam/polystyrene
  packing material
Plaster filler
Rubber hose pipe
Rubber plunger
Rawlplugs
Washers

How to get rid of it

Put an advertisement in your local paper.
Make it sound desirable.

Rent a stand at your local market.

Put an advertisement in your newsagent's
window.

Sell metals to a local scrap merchant.

Ask your friends if they want it.

If it is still useful but you can't carry it to your
local charity shop, ask a local charity with a
van to come and collect.

Take it to your local jumble sale.

Leave it on your doorstep with a 'Help Yourself' notice.

See if the dustmen will take it away.

Burn it in the garden.

Take it to the local council tip.

Dump bottles at local bottle bank for recycling. Your local authority will tell you where it is.

Call the refuse department at your local Town Hall. They will come and collect rubbish, for a fee.

Hire a skip. Look under Waste Disposal Services in your Yellow Pages.

Decide to keep it – and give it a facelift

Never dump an old fridge; children playing can get trapped inside, and suffocate.

Do you Know where they are?

Water Board stopcock. (Near or just inside the boundary of your property.)

The main stopcock. (Usually in kitchen area, in the airing cupboard or under the stairs.)

All other stopcocks in your home (and what they are for).

Cold water tank and the stopcock that isolates it from the piping system.

Central heating time switch.

Boiler thermostat.

Room thermostat(s).

Your main gas tap. (Usually near the main gas meter.)

Gas meter.

Fuse box.

Electricity meter.

Fire extinguisher. (Buy one now if you haven't got one.)

Your tool box.

Autumn check list

Check roof slates or tiles with binoculars – replace broken or missing ones.

Check guttering to see if it is blocked, broken or leaking – repair.

Check gutter outlets – clear of old leaves and general rubbish. Put a wire 'bird cage' on top of outlets to stop future blockages.

Check for leaning or cracking chimney stacks with binoculars – repair before Christmas Day!

Check if brickwork needs repointing.

Check outside woodwork and walls every 3–5 years to see if they need repainting.

Check that window frames and sills are not rotting and letting in damp.

Check that earth has not banked above damp-proof course – remove it.

Check for efflorescence (white powdery deposits) on internal and external walls.

Check against everything in *Hunt and destroy* (opposite).

Check your roof from inside the loft.

Check to see if internal pipes, especially those in an insulated loft, are sufficiently lagged.

Check for small plumbing leaks to lavatories, basins, baths and sinks.

Check drains to see if they need clearing.

Check if any taps are dripping – replace washers.

Check if radiators need draining – if they do, they'll be cold at the top and warm at the bottom.

Check that the mains stopcock can be turned off if necessary.

Check again and again for damp patches and mysterious stains.

Check throughout winter to ensure pipes don't freeze or burst.

Check and fill all wall, ceiling and floor cracks both indoors and out, except really large, persistent ones which may indicate foundation problems – phone surveyor.

Check for gaps between wall and bath/wall and sink – and re-grout.

Check to see through which doors and windows the wind is howling – fit draught excluders because it's going to get worse!

Check for broken and chipped panes of glass – replace.

Check none of your windows or doors is jammed – plane and re-paint if necessary.

Check for snapped sash cords – replace.

Check that burglar proofing system still works – have your burglar alarm serviced.

Check all electrical appliances work – have them serviced as well.

Check central heating works – call in a plumber to service the system before they are all heavily in demand!

Hunt and destroy...

Ants	Dry rot
Bats	Fleas
Bedbugs	Hornets
Black beetles	Lice
Bluebottles and other flies	Mice
	Mites (small spiders)
Cockroaches	Mosquitoes

Moths   Spiders
Rats   Wasps
Silverfish   Wet rot

Invaders Killer Kit

All-purpose   Moth deterrent
   insecticide aerosol   sachets
All-purpose   Mouse traps (use
   insecticide powder   chocolate, dried
Ant killer   fruit, nuts or lard)
Cat   Polythene (to wrap
Exterminators   clothes in)
Flea collar (for any   Town Hall (Public
   pet)   Health
Fumigators   Department)
Honey in jam jars (for   Vacuum cleaner
   wasps and bees)   Wood preservation
Insect repellent   company
Mouse poison   Woodworm killer

Preventing invaders

Keep your home clean, especially your kitchen. Brush walls and ceilings to prevent cobwebs.

Fill cracks in walls and floors.

Make sure dustbin lids fit tightly, and disinfect dustbins often.

Clean out food cupboards regularly.

Never store food or grain on the floor.

Avoid rotting animal or vegetable matter in the garden.

Put a mesh screen over open windows and doors.

Vacuum often. Vacuum underfelt and inside cupboards too, if you can.

Bag up all unused blankets, clothes, etc in polythene.

Clean and protect all stored articles, and inspect them regularly.

Remove clothes and linen from cupboards occasionally and shake them.

Check all second-hand furniture carefully for little woodworm holes.

Keep plumbing in good working order.

Try to ensure your home is not damp. Keep damp places well ventilated and make sure their condition is not deteriorating.

Keep a cat.

Clean your pets and their bedding regularly. Give them a flea collar, if appropriate.

Use insect repellent, moth balls and insecticide.

If your tap drips...

1. Find screwdriver, wrench or adjustable spanner, small spanner, pliers, the correct size washer and a cloth.

2. Turn water off at the mains.

3. Open tap and drain off all the water.

4. Put the cloth in the sink, in case you drop the tap.

5. Remove the tap handle, either by unscrewing the tiny screw at the side, or by pulling it off.

6. Wrap the same cloth around the body of the tap to protect it and pull it off or up to expose a large hexagonal nut.

7. Unscrew the nut with the spanner.

8. Lift free the inside part of the tap (the 'headgear').

9. You can now see the washer at the bottom, held by a small nut against a metal plate (the 'jumper plate').

10. With the small spanner, undo the small nut.

11. Remove the old washer.

12. Clean up any messy bits.

13. Fit the new washer with the maker's name facing downwards.

14. Replace the nut.

15. Re-assemble the tap.

16. Turn on the water supply.

17. Turn the tap on and off several times to check that it has stopped dripping.

If your Supatap drips...

1. Buy a new washer and jumper plate from a hardware store.

2. Find your adjustable spanner or wrench, a pencil and a nail brush.

3. Don't worry about turning the water off at the mains, you don't have to.

4. Open the tap a little, hold the nozzle firmly and undo the hexagonal nut with a spanner just above the spot you are holding.

5. Hold the loosened nut with one hand and, with the other hand, unscrew the entire nozzle anti-clockwise.

6. Insert a pencil into the end of the nozzle where the water normally comes out, and push out the washer piece and the jumper plate, both of which are in a 'flow straightener'.

7. Clean the flow straightener with the nail brush.

8. Pull out the washer plate and jumper.

9. Fit a new washer.

10. Re-assemble the tap.

Supatap is a modern-type tap which enables the washer to be changed without having to turn off the water supply. To aid recognition, most Supatap nozzles and handles are one piece, and point downwards into the sink.

If your sink is blocked...

1. Find a plunger, a cup and a rag.

2. Push rag into the basin overflow, so that air and water cannot escape when plunger is in use.

3. Using a cup, remove most of the water from the sink; leave about 25mm (1 inch).

4. Place plunger firmly over the plug hole.

5. Work plunger handle vigorously up and down.

6. When the blockage is dislodged, the water will drain out.

7. Turn on tap and repeat.

8. Remove rag from overflow hole.

9. Run cold water for a minute or two.

10. If using a plunger does not clear the sink, the blockage will have to be cleared from the trap or the waste pipe!

If appliances don't work...

Check that the plug is properly pushed into the socket.

Check that the appliance is switched on.

Check that the socket is switched on.

Check that the controls are properly set.

Check that the socket isn't broken by plugging the appliance into another socket.

Check that the plug is correctly wired.

Check that the fuse in the plug has not blown. Replace it.

Check the main fuse box to see if a fuse has blown. Replace it.

Check that there is not a power cut in your neighbourhood.

Check the flex of your appliance.

Check the appliance itself. Don't use it if it's broken.

If they still don't work...

Washing machine

Has the fuse blown?

Is the water turned on?

Are clothes loaded evenly?

Tumble dryer

Drying too slowly

Is your load too heavy?

Are your clothes too wet?

Is the fluff-collecting filter full?

Running noisily

Is the dryer resting unevenly on the floor?

Is the belt loose?

Vacuum cleaner

Has the fuse blown?

Is the dust bag too full?

Do you need a new bag?

Is the nozzle clogged?

Is the hose obstructed?

Toaster

Is mechanism jammed with crumbs?

Electric oven

Has the fuse blown?

Is the automatic oven control set at manual?

Dishwasher

Motor won't go

Has the fuse blown?

Is the drain hose kinked?

Is the impeller jammed with small pieces of food or broken glass?

Cleans badly

Are the dishes properly stacked?

If applicable, have you re-salted the machine recently?

Have you been using too much detergent?

Have you been using the recommended detergent?

Have you been using compatible detergent and water softener?

Refrigerator *Noisy*

Is fridge standing level and firmly?

Doesn't stay cold

Is the thermostat set too high?

Does the door seal need replacing?

Has the door been left open too long, too often?

Have you put shelf paper on the fridge shelves and prevented air circulating?

Food freezing

Is the thermostat set too low?

Is wrapping paper blocking the return air louvres in the freezer compartment?

Freezer Has the fuse blown?

Has the introduction of too much 'warm' food caused a temporary rise in temperature?

Did you leave the door open by mistake?

Is your thermostat setting too high?

Always read If appliances don't work (page 75) *first.*

Always switch the appliance off and pull the plug out of the socket before touching anything.

Never use an appliance you think may be broken; you could damage it further.

Always call the manufacturer's service department if you don't feel confident about checking the appliance yourself.

Always notice if the same fault recurs – either find out what you are doing wrong, or complain to the manufacturers.

How to wire a plug

1. Find a small screwdriver, wire stripper and cutter or a trimming knife.

2. Remove the plug cover by loosening the main screw on the underside.

3. Prise out the fuse.

4. Remove one flex clamp screw and loosen the other.

5. Unscrew the three tiny screws from the terminals, but don't take them out – you may lose them.

6. Cut away about 50mm (2 inches) of the outer sheath of the flex, be careful not to cut into the wires.

7. Fix the flex firmly under the clamp. The wire ends should reach about 13mm ($\frac{1}{2}$ inch) beyond the terminals.

8. Strip insulation from three wire ends to expose 6mm ($\frac{1}{4}$ inch) of wire for screw-hole terminals. Allow 13mm ($\frac{1}{2}$ inch) for clamp type terminals.

9. Twist the strands of wire and either insert into the holes (screw-hole terminals) or loop clockwise round terminals (clamp type).

10. Remember that the live wire is brown or red, the neutral wire is blue or black and the earth wire is green/yellow or green.

11. Check that no loose strands of wire remain.

12. Tighten screws.

13. Insert the correct fuse for the appliance.

14. Re-check that wires are on correct terminals.

15. Replace plug cover and tighten screw.

16. Shake the plug, if anything rattles, undo and start again!

Are you saving energy?

Insulation	Yes/No
Have you insulated your loft with at least 75mm (3 inches) of glass or mineral fibre, or 100mm (4 inches) of expanded polystyrene or any other granular insulation material?	
Have you got cavity walls (if your home is post 1920s, you probably have), and if so, are they insulated?	
Have you installed draught excluder strips around external doors and windows? Remember that in kitchens and bathrooms you need ventilation to prevent condensation and mould growth; also oil, gas or solid fuel appliances may need air to 'breathe'.	
Have you considered fitting double glazing?	
Have you checked floorboards and skirting boards for gaps and draughts and filled them with old newspaper?	
Have you tried to nail quadrant moulding round really draughty skirting?	
Have you got carpet underlay?	
Have you covered all solid concrete floors?	
Have you blocked off unused fireplaces and installed an air brick or grille to keep chimney free from condensation?	
Have you put a flap or box behind your letterbox to stop draughts?	

Heating   Yes/No

Do you limit full heating to one
room whenever possible?

Do you keep the sitting room
temperature no higher than 20°C
(68°F)?

Do you close curtains at night and
open them during the day?

Do you use heavy lined curtains?

Do you keep radiators clear of
curtains and furniture?

Do you have radiators on inside
rather than outside walls?

Do you have a sheet of aluminium
foil behind any radiator sited on
an outside wall?

Do you try and use less heat all
the time?

Do you put on another jumper
rather than turn up the heat?

Do you close doors of unused
rooms.

Do you have automatic door
closers on doors you use a lot?

Do you have your central heating
serviced regularly in summer or
autumn?

Do you replace worn parts of fires
and radiators immediately?

Do you replace old appliances
with more efficient new ones?

Do you use the poker gently on
open fires?

Water heating   Yes/No

Is the hot water cylinder insulated
with at least a 75mm (3 inch)
lagging jacket?

Is the cylinder thermostat set for
no higher than 55°C (130°F)?

Is the cold water tank lagged, and are all the water pipes in the loft?

Is the immersion heater switched off when not in use, or has a time switch been installed?

Is the hot water tap always turned off properly, and have you checked to ensure no hot water taps are dripping?

Is the shower rather than the bath used whenever possible?

Is the washing up bowl used in the kitchen sink for washing up rather than a running hot tap?

Is the dishwasher used only when full?

Cooking	Yes/No

Do you match saucepans to ring sizes?

Do you try and cook more than one vegetable in a pot?

Do you put close-fitting lids on saucepans?

Do you turn heat down once contents boil?

Do you have an automatic electric kettle?

Do you boil only the amount of liquid you need and no more?

Do you use a pressure cooker?

Do you make maximum use of oven shelf-space?

Do you avoid opening the oven door when cooking?

Do you use a toaster rather than the grill for toast?

Do you avoid pre-heating the oven unless fast-browning?

Refrigerator and freezer   Yes/No

Is the refrigerator/freezer door/lid
opened only when absolutely
necessary?

Is the refrigerator/freezer
defrosted regularly?

Is the freezer at least three-
quarters full?

Is the food, if hot, allowed to cool
down before being put in the
refrigerator or freezer?

Is the 'fast freeze' left on for no
longer than necessary?

Is the temperature set no lower
than necessary?

Is the refrigerator/freezer
serviced regularly?

Laundry   Yes/No

Do you only use the washing
machine when you have a full
load?

Do you wash least-soiled clothes
first when using a twin-tub
washing machine?

Do you soak heavily soiled
clothes in enzyme detergent first
to shorten wash time?

Do you reduce the water content
of the clothes as much as
possible before loading them into
a tumble dryer?

Do you iron only when necessary?
(Many man-made fabrics don't
require ironing.)

Lighting   Yes/No

Are you turning off lights that are
not in use?

Are you using bright lights where
essential and low wattage bulbs
elsewhere?

	Yes/No
Are you using fluorescent lamps where possible?	
Are you using dimmer switches?	
Are you using outdoor lights only when necessary?	
Are you using one large rather than several small bulbs?	

Entertainment	Yes/No
Is the TV, stereo and radio turned off when not being watched or listened to?	

Did you answer 'Yes' to all (or most) questions?

Be careful about making too many temperature reductions in places where there are old people or young babies.

Be careful about turning off all lights when nobody is at home or the dark might invite burglars. See Anti-burglar quiz *(page 118).*

Have appliances regularly serviced.

Powercut planning

Buy candles, matches, torches and batteries or a dynamo torch and keep in strategic places!

For sophisticated lighting, buy oil and hurricane lamps.

If you have a real fire, stock up on wood and coal.

Buy a paraffin heater, and remember to ventilate room well when using it.

Insure freezer contents.

Buy a camping cooker.

If you know of powercut beforehand, make hot water bottles and fill vacuum flasks with hot water.

When powercut starts, switch off and unplug all electrical appliances, but leave several lights on so that you can tell when power is restored.

Move portable heaters away from furniture and curtains to avoid the risk of fire when electricity is restored.

Don't open fridge or freezer door more than necessary.

Wear warm clothing if cold, and move around a lot.

Be careful with candles.

Don't move oil or paraffin heaters when alight.

When power is restored, examine all frozen food and eat any thawed food first. Do not re-freeze thawed food.

Drain the dishwasher and washing machine and re-start programmes.

Remember to reset all electric clocks, automatic timers on cookers and central heating timers.

Eating

Basic kitchen equipment

Several sharp knives
Knife sharpener
 (carbon steel)
Stainless steel fruit
 knife (serrated
 edge)
Palette-knife
Wooden spoons
Large metal spoon
Large perforated
 spoon
Fish slice
Spatula with rubber
 blade
Ladle
Whisk
Food mixer
Potato peeler
Potato masher
Corkscrew
Bottle opener
Can opener
Kitchen scissors
Grater (four-sided
 with handle)
Garlic press
Lemon squeezer
Salt and pepper
 mills
Measuring spoons
Measuring jug
Standard size cup
 (for American
 recipes)
Scales
Rolling pin
Pastry brush
Nylon sieve
Stainless steel sieve

Metal colander
Assorted sizes of
 pudding basins
2 large mixing bowls
Wooden chopping
 board
Automatic electric
 kettle
Kitchen timer
Oven gloves
Apron
Fire extinguisher

Pots and pans
3 different size
 saucepans (with
 lids)
2 frying pans (one
 with lid)
Roasting tin
2 casseroles
Various sizes of loaf
 tins
2 sandwich tins
Cake tin (deep)
2 jam tart tins
2 tin pie plates
Flan tins (one for 4–6
 people, one for 8–
 10 people)
2 baking sheets
Cake cooling tray (or
 grill rack)
Pie dish
2 soufflé dishes
2 gratin dishes
Double boiler
Omelette pan
Deep fat frying pan

... *and a radio, lots of work surfaces, a comfortable chair and an enormous dustbin!*

Specialised utensils

Apple corer
Basting spoon
Biscuit cutters
Bread knife
Carving knife and
 fork
Coffee grinder
Coffee-making
 machine
Egg pricker
Egg slicer
Fat syringe
Flour sifter
Funnel
Grapefruit knife
Ice-cream scoop
Ice trays
Jelly mould

Juice presser
Lettuce spinner
Liquidiser
Mandoline
Meat basher
Melon baller
Mincer
Nutcracker
Pastry cutters
Pie funnel
Piping bag with
 various nozzles
Salad servers
Skewers (meat and
 kebab)
Storage jars
Tea strainer
Toaster

Cordon Bleu cooks love a...

Balloon whisk
Brioche mould
Clay cooker/oven
 brick
Cook book stand
Copper bowl (for
 beating egg
 whites)
Copper pans (set of
 thick-bottomed
 ones)
Espresso coffee
 maker
Fish kettle
 (aluminium)
Fondue pot
Food processor
Herb garden (See
 Easy indoor herbs,
 page 142.)

Ice-cream maker
Knife rack
Marble slab (for
 pastry or fondant
 icing)
Oyster opener
Pestle and mortar
Preserving pan
Pressure cooker
Shears (heavy ones
 for poultry, etc)
Spice rack
Sugar and roasting
 thermometers
Vegetable steamer
Waffle iron
Wok plus chopper
Yoghurt maker

. . . and a cookery course!

Complete china cupboard

Soup plates
Bouillon bowls
Soup tureen
Dinner plates
Intermediate plates
Side plates
Dessert plates
Serving dishes
Platters
Salad or serving bowl
Gravy/sauce boats
  with stands
Egg cups
Butter dish

Jam pots
Cups
Saucers
Tea pot
Milk jug
Sugar bowls
Demi-tasse cups
Demi-tasse saucers
Coffee pot
Cream jug
Mugs
Jugs (of varying
  sizes)

If you don't want a matching set, try buying different designs in the same colour.

Each china or earthenware service comes with different pieces. This list is a complete list, but don't expect all sets to contain all pieces.

Complete silver service

Soup spoons
Soup ladles
Fish knives and forks
Fish slice
Large knives and
  forks
Steak knives
Carving set
Serving spoons and
  forks
Platters
Cream or sauce ladle
Gravy/sauce boat
  and tray
Salt and pepper
shakers
Mustard bowl
Small knives
Butter knife

Dessert spoons and
  forks
Fruit knives and forks
Cake forks
Sundae spoons
Cake or pie server
Fruit/chocolate bowls
Marmalade/jam
  spoon
Honey spoon
Tray
Napkin rings
Teaspoons
Tea pot
Sugar bowl
Milk jug
Tea strainer
Sugar sifter
Sugar tongs

Coffee spoons
Coffee pot
Cream jug
Candlesticks
Cigarette box

Cocktail shaker
Cocktail spoon
Pickle forks
Ice bucket

The pieces included in a silver service will depend very much on the date of its manufacture and design.

Complete glass cupboard

Water tumblers
Red wine glasses
White wine glasses
Hock glasses (brown
  or green stemmed)
Champagne flutes
Sherry/port/liqueur
  glasses
Martini glasses
Brandy balloons
Whisky tumblers

Range of cocktail
  glasses
Large jugs/pitchers
Claret jug
Port decanter
Sherry/gin/whisky
  decanters (square
  shaped)
Dessert bowls
Finger bowls
Vases

Basic store cupboard

Fridge
Milk
Eggs
Butter
Margarine
Cheese
Yoghurt

Herbs and spices
Basil (with tomatoes)
Bay leaves (in soups,
  stews, etc)
Chili powder (for hot
  dishes)
Cinnamon (try with
  baked bananas)

Cloves (with cooked
  apples)
Curry powder (in
  soups,
  mayonnaise, etc)
Nutmeg (on onion
  and celery
  soup)
Oregano (in Italian
  dishes)
Paprika pepper (in
  goulash and as
  garnish)
Rosemary (better
  fresh, but for pork,
  veal, etc)

Sage (on pork or in
  stuffings)
Tarragon (with fish,
  chicken, etc)
Thyme (try on pork
  chops)
Whole black
  peppercorns
  (essential)
Fresh garlic (for
  flavour)

Dry goods
Cereals/muesli
Flour
Baking powder
Cornflour
Sugar (assorted)
Olive oil
Cooking oil
Salt and pepper
Mustard (assorted)
Wine vinegar
Concentrated lemon
  juice
Stock cubes

Worcestershire
  sauce
Tomato purée
Pickles and relishes
Peanuts
Packets of dried
  soup
Crispbreads
Pasta and rice
Canned salmon/tuna
Canned kidney
  beans
Canned tomatoes
Sweet biscuits
Currants and
  sultanas
Custard powder
Gelatine
Strawberry (or other)
  jam
Marmalade
Honey
Tea
Coffee beans
Squash
Cocoa

Cordon Bleu store cupboard

Fridge
Mineral water
Orange/grapefruit
  juice

Herbs and spices
Bouquet garni (for
  flavouring soups,
  stews, etc)
Cardamom (black
  and green)
Cayenne pepper (for
  chilis and other hot
  foods)
Chervil (use with fish)
Cinnamon (stick)
Coriander (for curries

and stuffings)
Cummin (try in
  beetroot soup)
Dill (with cucumber
  salads and fish)
Garam Masala (for
  Oriental cooking)
Ginger (for melon
  and gingercake)
Green peppercorns
  (for flavouring
  sauces)
Juniper berries (for
  pâtés, especially
  game)
Mace (for sauces)
Marjoram (for

stuffings and tomato dishes)
Sea salt (for your salt mill)
Turmeric (for rice and curries)
Vanilla pods (leave one in a jar of caster sugar)
Fresh parsley, mint, rosemary, etc

Dry goods
Canned pâté
Olives
Canned anchovies
Cans of lobster bisque, game soup and other exotic soups
Brown rice
Canned pimentos
Canned consommé (for sauces)
Dried Italian mushrooms (use in bolognese sauce)
Canned artichoke hearts

Canned button mushrooms
Dried pulses
Nut oil
Soy sauce
Redcurrant jelly
Mango chutney
Parmesan cheese
Vanilla essence
Almond essence
Arrowroot
Nibbed/flaked/ ground almonds
Hazelnuts
Walnuts
Good plain chocolate for cooking
Dried apricots
Home-made marmalade
Crème de marron
Earl Grey and Lapsan Suchong tea
Freeze-dried coffee
Cooking wine, red and white
Cooking brandy
Marsala
Kirsch

This list presumes that you already have the Basic store cupboard *(page 89) collection. Alter list according to your palate.*

Emergency freezer contents

Chops
Sausages
Minced beef
Bacon
Chicken and meat stock
Oven chips
Peas
Sweetcorn

Brussels sprouts
Broccoli
Spinach
Shortcrust pastry
Puff pastry
Ice cream (exotic flavours)
Bread (sliced)

*Stock can be kept in ice cube trays if you only
need a little at a time. Sliced bread can be
toasted straight from the freezer.*

Food in season in January

Vegetables
Artichoke, Jerusalem
Broccoli
Brussels sprouts
Celery
Chicory
Leeks
Parsnips
Potatoes, new
Red cabbage
Spring greens
Swedes

Fruit
Cranberries
Rhubarb
Seville oranges

Poultry & Game
Goose
Rabbit
Turkey
Hare
Partridge
Pheasant
Wild duck
Wild goose

Fish
Carp
Cod
Haddock
Hake
Halibut
Herring
Mussels
Oysters
Pike
Scallops
Skate
Sole
Sprats

Food in season in February

Vegetables
Artichoke, Jerusalem
Broccoli
Brussels sprouts
Celery
Chicory
Leeks
Parsnips
Potatoes, new
Red cabbage
Spring greens
Swedes

Fruit
Rhubarb

Poultry & Game
Goose
Rabbit
Turkey
Hare
Wild duck

Fish
Carp

Cod
Haddock
Hake
Halibut
Herring
Mussels
Oysters

Pike
Salmon
Scallops
Skate
Sole
Sprats
Whitebait

Food in season in March

Vegetables
Artichoke, globe
Artichoke, Jerusalem
Broccoli
Brussels sprouts
Chicory
Leeks
Parsnips
Potatoes, new
Spinach
Spring greens
Swedes

Fruit
Rhubarb

Poultry & Game
Goose
Turkey

Fish
Carp
Hake
Halibut
Herring
Mussels
Oysters
Pike
Salmon
Salmon trout
Scallops
Skate
Sole
Sprats
Trout
Turbot
Whitebait

Food in season in April

Vegetables
Artichoke, globe
Broccoli
Chicory
Leeks
Parsnips
Potatoes, new
Spinach
Spring greens
Swedes

Fruit
Rhubarb

Poultry & Game
Turkey

Fish
Brill
Crayfish
Lobster

Mackerel	Trout
Oysters	Turbot
Salmon	Whitebait
Salmon trout	

Food in season in May

Vegetables
Artichoke, globe
Asparagus
Courgettes
Spinach
Spring greens

Fruit
Apricots
Gooseberries
Rhubarb
Strawberries

Fish
Brill
Crab
Crayfish
Haddock
Herring
Lobster
Mackerel
Mullet
Salmon
Salmon trout
Sole
Trout
Turbot
Whitebait

Food in season in June

Vegetables
Artichoke, globe
Asparagus
Beans, broad
Beans, French
Courgettes
Peas
Spinach

Fruit
Apricots
Black currants
Cherries
Gooseberries
Red currants
Rhubarb
Strawberries

Fish
Brill
Carp
Crab
Crayfish
Haddock
Herring
Lobster
Mackerel
Mullet
Salmon
Salmon trout
Sole
Trout
Turbot
Whitebait

Food in season in July

Vegetables
Beans, broad
Beans, French
Beans, runner
Courgettes
Peas
Spinach

Fruit
Apricots
Black currants
Cherries
Gooseberries
Greengages
Loganberries
Raspberries
Red currants
Rhubarb
Strawberries

Poultry & Game
Venison

Fish
Brill
Carp
Crab
Crayfish
Haddock
Hake
Halibut
Herring
Lobster
Mullet
Salmon
Salmon trout
Sole
Trout
Turbot
Whitebait

Food in season in August

Vegetables
Beans, broad
Beans, French
Beans, runner
Corn on the cob
Courgettes
Marrow
Peas
Spinach

Fruit
Blackberries
Black currants
Greengages
Peaches
Pears
Plums
Raspberries
Red currants

Poultry & Game
Grouse
Venison

Fish
Brill
Carp
Crab
Crayfish
Haddock
Hake
Halibut
Herring
Lobster
Mullet
Pike
Salmon
Salmon trout
Sole
Trout
Turbot

Food in season in September

Vegetables
Beans, French
Beans, runner
Celery
Corn on the cob
Courgettes
Leeks
Marrow
Parsnips
Spinach

Fruit
Blackberries
Damsons
Peaches
Pears
Plums
Raspberries

Poultry & Game
Grouse
Hare
Partridge
Venison
Wild duck

Fish
Carp
Crayfish
Dab
Haddock
Hake
Halibut
Herring
Lobster
Mullet
Mussels
Oysters
Pike
Sole
Trout

Food in season in October

Vegetables
Artichoke, Jerusalem
Broccoli
Brussels sprouts
Celery
Chicory
Leeks
Parsnips
Red cabbage
Spinach
Spring greens
Swedes

Fruit
Cranberries
Pears

Poultry & Game
Goose
Grouse
Hare
Partridge
Pheasant
Rabbit
Turkey
Venison
Wild duck
Wild goose

Fish
Carp
Cod
Haddock
Hake
Halibut
Herring
Mussels
Oysters

Pike
Scallops
Skate

Sole
Sprats

Food in season in November

Vegetables
Beans, runner
Broccoli
Brussels sprouts
Celery
Leeks
Marrow
Parsnips
Red cabbage
Spinach
Swedes

Fruit
Blackberries
Damsons
Pears

Poultry & Game
Goose
Grouse
Hare

Partridge
Pheasant
Rabbit
Venison
Wild duck

Fish
Carp
Cod
Haddock
Hake
Halibut
Herring
Lobster
Mullet
Mussels
Oysters
Pike
Skate
Sole

Food in season in December

Vegetables
Artichoke, Jerusalem
Broccoli
Brussels sprouts
Celery
Chicory
Leeks
Parsnips
Red cabbage
Spinach
Swedes

Fruit
Cranberries
Pears

Poultry & Game
Goose
Grouse
Hare
Partridge
Pheasant
Rabbit

Turkey
Venison
Wild duck
Wild goose

Fish
Carp
Cod
Haddock
Hake

Halibut
Herring
Mussels
Oysters
Pike
Scallops
Skate
Sole
Sprats

The fruit and vegetables given in the above lists are all home-grown produce and are seasonal, even though they may be available in shops all year round. The lists show when they are in season. Most fish can be bought all year round. The lists show when certain fish are of better quality and more plentiful.

Food quantities per person

Meat

Meat	
Minced meat	175g (6oz)
Beef, lamb, pork with bone	225g (8oz)
Beef, lamb, pork without bone	175g (6oz)

Poultry, on the bone

Poultry, on the bone	
Chicken (roast)	275g (10oz)
Chicken (boiled)	400g (14oz)
Duck	450g (1lb)
Turkey	450g (1lb)

Game

Game	
Venison	225g (8oz)
Rabbit	275g (10oz)
Pheasant, one bird	quarter to a half
Partridge (young)	one bird
Quail	one bird

Fish

Headless, skinned and cleaned, with bones	225g (8oz)
With head, bones, skin and tail	450g (1lb)
Smoked, with bones	225g (8oz)
Smoked, filleted	175g (6oz)
Fillets	175g (6oz)

Shellfish

Crab, in shell	350g (12oz)
Lobster, in shell	225g (8 oz)
Mussels	425ml ($\frac{3}{4}$ pint)
Shrimps, peeled	100g (4oz)
Oysters, fresh as starter	at least 6
Escargot, as starter	6

Pasta, rice and pulses

Rice	50g (2oz)
Lentils	50g (2oz)
Pasta, as main course	100g (4oz)
Beans	50g (2oz)

Vegetables

Asparagus	350g (12oz)
Cabbage	175g (6oz)
Carrots	175g (6oz)
Green beans	275g (10oz)
Peas, in pod	225g (8oz)
Potatoes (old)	450g (1lb)
Potatoes (new)	225g (8oz)
Spinach	275g (10oz)

Onions without tears

Try singing at the same time.
Try chilling the onion in the fridge first.
Try sucking a teaspoon.
Try standing in a draught.
Try holding the onion under cold running water.
Try breathing in through your mouth and out through your nose.
Try sticking a piece of bread on the point of the knife.
Try holding the onion at eye level.
Try not wiping your eyes if they water.
Try not bending over the onion.
Try doing it often enough to become immune.

Vegetable cooking times

Asparagus (steamed/boiled)	10–15 mins
Broad beans (boiled)	7–10 mins
French beans (boiled)	8–12 mins
Runner beans (boiled)	7–10 mins
Broccoli (boiled)	10–20 mins
Broccoli, sprouting (boiled)	8–15 mins
Brussels sprouts (boiled)	6–12 mins
Cabbage, red (stewed with cover)	2–3 hours (until soft)
Cabbage, spring (stir-fry) (boiled)	10 mins 5 mins
Carrots (boiled)	10–15 mins
Cauliflower (boiled)	12 mins

Courgettes (sweated in butter)	20 mins
Jerusalem artichokes (steamed/boiled)	30–40 mins
Leeks (boiled)	10–15 mins
Mange-tout peas (stir fry/boiled/sweated)	5 mins
Marrow (steamed/baked)	30 mins
Mushrooms (sweated in butter)	4–8 mins
Onions (boiled) (steamed) (baked)	15–30 mins 20–40 mins $1-1\frac{1}{2}$ hours
Peas (boiled)	10–15 mins
Potatoes (roasted) (other methods)	$1\frac{1}{2}$ hours up to 30 mins
Potatoes, new (steamed/boiled)	15–30 mins
Shallots (steamed/boiled)	15–30 mins
Spinach (in covered saucepan with no water)	4 mins
Turnips (steamed/sweated)	20–30 mins

Presentation tips

Do try pouring cream in the centre of a bowl of tomato soup and quickly swirling the soup with a spoon.

Do try adding croûtons to soup for a farmhouse look.

Do try scoring the bottom of a radish or spring onion and putting it in iced water for an unusual garnish.

Do try sprinkling cress over a salad.

Do, for an original fish garnish, cut a lime or lemon into circular slices, then cut from the centre of each slice to the edge and twist.

Do arrange semi-circular slices of lemon,

orange and lime alternately along the side of a dish.

Do try sprinkling chopped parsley or chives in symmetrical lines over food for an elegant effect.

Do, before cooking, try scoring a lamb roast and placing sprigs of fresh rosemary in the cuts.

Do try piping mashed potato in a swirl on top of a thick stew and browning it quickly in the oven.

Do try sprinkling alternate lines of sieved hard-boiled egg yolk and chopped parsley on a meat loaf.

Do try draping very finely sliced lemon rind over the whipped cream decorating a lemon mousse. (Remember to boil the rind for a few minutes first to remove the bitter taste).

Do try the same with orange.

Do keep garnishes edible, fresh and subdued.

Do make sure garnishes heighten taste and colour, either through contrast or similarity.

Do try to choose a serving dish of an appropriate shape and size, such as a long thin platter for whole fish.

Do serve plain food on patterned or coloured plates and, conversely, multi-coloured and complicated food on plain plates.

Don't present a sparsely covered plate of food; fill the plate up and if there isn't enough food, use a smaller plate.

Don't, however, overload guests' plates; they can always ask for more.

Do try serving a pre-dinner dip with chicory leaves for a change.

Do try serving salad on a red cabbage leaf.

Do serve medium-sized chunks of two different cheeses on your cheese board rather than lots of small pieces.

Oven temperatures

Oven	°F	°C	Gas Mark
Very cool	225–250	110–120	$\frac{1}{4}-\frac{1}{2}$
Cool	275–300	140–150	1–2
Warm	325	160	3
Moderate	350	180	4
Fairly hot	375–400	190–200	5–6
Hot	425	220	7
Very hot	450–475	230–240	8–9

To convert Centigrade to Fahrenheit, divide by 5, multiply by 9 and then add 32; to convert Fahrenheit to Centigrade, subtract 32, divide by 9 and multiply by 5.

Ounces to grams

Ounces (oz)	Grams (g)
1	28 (approx 25g)
2	56 (approx 50g)
3	85 (approx 75g)
4	113 (approx 100g or 125g)
5	142 (approx 150g)
6	170 (approx 175g)
7	198 (approx 200g)
8	227 (approx 225g)
12	340 (approx 350g)
1lb	454 (approx 450g)
1$\frac{1}{2}$lb	680 (approx 675g)
2lb	907 (approx 900g)
3lb	1.36kg (approx 1.4kg)
4lb	1.81kg (approx 1.8kg)
5lb	2.27kg (approx 2.3kg)

sleeping

Sleeping Kit

Comfortable bed(s)

Per bed (traditional)
3 pairs of sheets
3–4 blankets
Eiderdown

Per bed (using duvet)
3 fitted sheets
2 valances
1 duvet
3 duvet covers

Per bed (either case)
2 undersheets

Pillows (as many as you like)
Under pillowcase per pillow
3 pillowcases per pillow
Bedcover
1 electric blanket
Hot water bottle (not to be used with electric blanket)
Bedside table(s)
Bedside lamp(s)
Good book(s)
Radio alarm!

Electric blanket care

Always follow the manufacturer's instructions, both for using and cleaning the blanket.

Never plug an electric blanket into an adapter being used for another appliance.

Never plug an electric blanket into a light fitting as it may be switched on unintentionally.

Never use an underblanket as an overblanket, or vice versa.

Always tie an underblanket securely to the mattress.

Never use a blanket folded or creased.

Never stick pins into an electric blanket.

Never use the blanket if it is wet.

Never switch on the blanket to help it dry out, let it dry naturally.

Never use a hot water bottle with an electric blanket in case the bottle leaks.

Always be careful about using an electric

blanket in the beds of children or elders if there is likelihood of incontinence.

Always roll or fold overblankets with the minimum number of creases. Store in a dry place, or leave flat on a spare bed. Underblankets can be left tied to the bed all year round.

Always check frequently for frayed edges, loose connections at the plug and controls, fabric wear, scorch marks, damage to the flexible cord and displaced heating wires.

Always have the blanket regularly serviced and, if there are any signs of wear or damage, return the blanket to the manufacturer.

Hints for insomniacs

Imagine you are going over the Niagara Falls on a log of wood the width of your foot.

Count backwards from 1,000 to 0, subtracting 7 every time.

Repeat the same word or phrase over and over again until you fall asleep.

Relax each part of your body in turn, starting with your feet and working upwards.

Breathe deeply and regularly, as you would when asleep. If your partner is asleep, copy his or her breathing pattern and relax.

If you are alone, lie on your back with your eyes shut and recite a poem – very softly.

Turn on the light and pick up that boring book.

Get up and have a cup of hot milk, sweetened with honey, and an aspirin.

Make sure you're warm enough – get a hot water bottle or another blanket if you are cold.

Stop snoring !

Talk to him (or her!)
Pinch his nose gently – if you think he won't get upset.
Whistle.
Turn him onto his side.
Gently nudge him repeatedly.
Put a knotted handkerchief down the back of his pyjamas – to force him to lie on his side.
If the worst comes to the worst, wear earplugs.

safety

Safety in the home

Aerosol cans: Keep away from heat; don't puncture or incinerate as they can explode.

Backs: Be careful when lifting heavy items; bend your knees. Get help.

Baths: For elders, use a non-slip mat in the bath and fit grip-handles. Always run cold water into the bath first and check water temperature before stepping in. Never leave a child under three alone in the bath.

Cars: Never leave the engine running in the garage as exhaust fumes can be deadly in an enclosed space.

Carpets: Replace worn carpets or move them so that the worn section is under a piece of furniture; be careful on stairs as holes can cause accidents.

Chemicals: Never leave chemicals lying around and never decant them into soft drinks containers. Read and follow instructions before using.

Children: See *Keep your children safe* (page 160).

Cleaning agents: If you have young children, lock up all cleaning agents. Always follow instructions.

Elders: See *Keep your elders safe* (page 162).

Electricity: See *Safety with electricity* (page 112).

Equipment: Service equipment regularly.

Fire: See *Guard against fire* (page 114).

Floors: Never polish floors so well that you slip; use non-slip floor polish and fix rugs, mats, etc to the floor.

Gas: See *Being safe with gas* (page 110).

Knives: Keep knives stored away from children. Always carry knives with points facing downwards.

Ladders: Use a ladder instead of balancing on chair arm or pile of books.

Light: Make sure paths, stairs, landings, etc

are always well lit.

Manufacturers: Always read and follow manufacturer's instructions.

Medicines: See *Medicine cupboard check* (page 180).

Mirrors: Make sure the bathroom mirror is well lit, so you (or your partner) don't cut your face shaving or put make-up on unevenly!

Paint: Use non-toxic paint, especially in the nursery.

Plastic bags: Keep well away from children.

Television: Never remove the back of your television set, even if it is unplugged.

Tools: Always carry sharp tools with points facing downwards. Never leave tools lying around.

Weeds: Remove all poisonous plants (deadly nightshade, laburnum, hemlock, yew, toadstools, etc), or keep children away from them.

You: Know your limitations. Never be afraid or embarrassed to ask for help and/or advice should you need it.

Being safe with gas

Make sure gas appliances have the British Gas Seal of Approval or the BSI/QAC Safety Mark.

Be careful when buying second-hand gas appliances. If you have any doubts, don't buy.

Read all instruction manuals carefully. (Make sure that when you move you leave the manuals for next occupier, and check that they are left for you.)

Only install gas appliances or carry out any work on your gas system yourself if you are a specialist. It could be dangerous.

If you are worried about any of your appliances, have them checked by your local gas service.

Service gas central heating, water heaters and fires once a year.

Service all other gas appliances every two years.

If you notice discoloration or staining on the wall next to your gas fire or water heater, stop using it and call the gas service.

Clean your gas cooker regularly. Flames should burn blue, with a clearly defined paler blue cone in the centre.

Never turn on gas rings or oven without lighting gas.

Always turn oven and rings off after use.

Make sure pilot lights never go out.

Never block ventilators either in doors, windows or walls. Gas appliances must breathe.

Never check for gas leaks with a naked flame.

Don't use water heater while in the bath unless it is a heater of the room-sealed type.

Don't shut both door and window while running bath water unless you have a balanced flue water heater.

Fit fixed fire guards around gas fires (if there are children or old people around).

If you smell gas...

Put out your cigarette. Never check for a gas leak with a match or any other naked flame.

Do not operate electrical switches (including doorbells). Do not turn them either on or off.

Open windows and doors to get rid of gas.

See if a gas tap has been left on accidentally or if a pilot light has gone out.

If you suspect a gas leak, turn off the supply at the main gas tap and call the local gas service. (Look under 'Gas' in your telephone directory.)

If you can't turn off the supply or if the smell continues, you must call the gas service immediately or ask someone else to do so.

If you smell gas, report it.

Safety with electricity

Look for the BEAB (British Electro-Technical Approvals Board) mark of safety on everything you buy.

Only buy good quality plugs, light fittings, heaters, etc.

Make sure plugs are correctly wired.

Fit the correct fuse for the appliance and never replace a cartridge fuse with fuse wire, even as a temporary measure.

Use brown 13-amp fuses for appliances over 750 watts and red 3-amp fuses for appliances under 750 watts (such as lights, hair-dryers, radios).

Buy safety covers for sockets or use plugs with part-insulated pins (if you have young children).

Replace cracked and chipped plugs and sockets immediately.

Check that all adapters have fuses.

Use adapters as little as possible; if you regularly use an adapter on a socket, change the socket to a double.

Never plug flex directly into a socket, always use a plug.

Never work with wet or worn flex.

Use short flexes so that you do not trip over them.

Always use a single length of flex from plug to appliance; avoid joins.

Never staple a flex to the wall or skirting board.

Never run a flex under carpet or linoleum.

Never let a flex touch hot fires, toasters, cookers, irons, etc, or go near the blades of a fan, lawnmower, etc.

Always when lawn-mowing or ironing make sure the flex comes from behind you and goes over your shoulder, rather than lying on the grass in front of the mower or on the ironing board under the iron.

Make sure all metal light fittings, including standard and table lamps, use a three-core flex and have an earth connection.

Never run an electric appliance from a lamp fitting.

Never exceed the maximum wattage recommended on fittings and lampshades.

Always switch lights off before changing light bulbs, and let bulbs cool before removing.

Always unplug an electrical appliance before examining or cleaning it.

Always, if working on fixed electrical equipment, switch electricity off at mains.

Never touch electrical equipment with wet hands.

Never fit a wall switch or a socket outlet in a bathroom. Fit pull-cord switches for lights and heaters, fit a special permanent shaver socket with isolating transformer for shavers.

Never use a portable electrical appliance in a bathroom, even if it is plugged in outside.

Always unplug a steam iron before filling it.

Keep any outdoor socket outlets under cover or use a special waterproof box.

Shield airing cupboard heaters against falling clothes and make sure they have an overheat cut-out.

Never cover or obstruct the air grilles on your fan heater.

Never drape clothes or towels over a heater,

unless it is specifically made for drying clothes.

Make sure radiant fires have permanent safety guards.

Fix radiant fires high on the wall in small rooms, and place at least 1 metre (3 feet) from furniture, curtain or doors.

Never fit a time switch or delay control to a radiant fire.

Make sure time-switched heaters are positioned well clear of curtains, furnishings, etc.

Try and check appliances every time you use them.

Have major appliances checked annually.

Have house wiring tested every five years; check the earthing system.

Have wiring renewed if more than 25 years old, or if socket outlets are the round-pin type.

Make sure any faults in your electrical appliances are corrected immediately.

Always call an electrician if fuses blow repeatedly, or if your television goes wrong whenever your fridge breaks down.

Call in an expert for electrical repairs and wiring.

See also Guard against fire *(below)*.

Guard against fire

Adhesives, strippers, thinners and other chemicals: Follow instructions carefully. Keep windows open and avoid naked lights when using.

Alarms: Get fire warning devices fitted.

Appliances: All gas and electrical appliances should be BEAB/BSI approved and serviced regularly.

Blankets, carpets, etc: Check to see if fabrics are flame-resistant before buying.

Bonfires: Keep bonfires well away from fences, bushes, outhouses, etc. Be careful when lighting (don't use petrol or paraffin), and never leave children alone near them.

Chimneys: Sweep regularly to stop soot, etc catching light.

Chip pans: Never fill your chip pan more than $\frac{1}{3}$ full of cooking oil, or $\frac{2}{3}$ full when food is added. Make sure chip pan completely covers electric ring or gas flame.

Cigarettes: Never smoke in bed or in your garage or workshop. Make sure you have enough ashtrays and don't flick ash onto the floor.

Clothes: Only dry clothes on or above a heater that has been specifically designed for the purpose.

Curtains: Never site your cooker near a curtained window. Never place electric or oil heaters near a curtain.

Electric blankets: See *Electric blanket care* (page 105). Never use your electric blanket when damp or folded, and switch underblankets off before getting into bed.

Extinguisher: Very useful – but your family (and you) must know how to use it.

Fire lighters: Are they safely stored?

Fondue pots: Make sure that you always put a metal dish underneath the fondue pot to catch overflowing alcohol.

Frying pans: Make sure that your family knows that 'grease' fires should never be put out with water? Do you have a smother blanket or suitable extinguisher in the kitchen?

Guards: All open fires should have a guard in front of them. If you have young children, install a guard that fixes to the wall.

Ignorance: Make sure that your family knows what to do in the event of fire. Do they all know the number of the fire brigade?

Irons: Never walk away from an iron which is

turned on. Take the phone off the hook when you are ironing, or bring it to the ironing board. Or simply turn off the iron when the phone rings.

Lawnmowers: Is the petrol can stored in a safe place?

Matches: Have you taught your children how to use them properly?

Mirrors: Never hang mirrors over fireplaces – you might be tempted to stand too close to the open fire to look at yourself in it.

Oil heaters: Only use oil heaters that automatically cut off when tipped over. Never carry them when alight.

Paraffin: Keep a drip tray under paraffin container to retain any spillage. Store paraffin in an outhouse.

Tea towels: Never leave them to dry over your hob.

Tiles: Never paint polystyrene tiles with gloss—it is an inflammable combination.

Water: Never touch anything electrical with wet hands. Keep electrical appliances out of bathrooms and away from sinks.

Windows: Don't site your gas stove near a window as a draught could extinguish a lit burner or pilot light.

Wiring: Have your wiring inspected by experts every five years. Read *Safety with electricity* (page 112).

If a fire starts

Everyone in the house should go to the ground floor (to a previously arranged place), from where they can leave the building safely.

Call the fire brigade at once. Do it yourself – never rely on anybody else to do so.

Before investigating the fire, make sure everyone else is safe and that the fire brigade has been called.

Try to reduce any draughts which may fan the fire. Close all doors and windows, even in rooms away from the fire.

Position somebody outside the house to wave at the fire brigade when it arrives so the driver can locate the fire quickly.

If necessary, evacuate the house and shut the front door behind you.

Remember, if you must go back inside to find someone, cover your face with a wet cloth to protect your lungs.

Do make sure that your family has a plan for evacuating the home in case of a fire.

See *Safety with electricity* (page 112), and *Being safe with gas* (page 110).

If cut off by fire

Close the door of the room you are in and any fanlight or other opening to the rest of the building.

Block up any cracks with bedding etc.

Open the window and try to attract attention by shouting at anyone passing by.

If the room fills with smoke, lean out of the window – unless prevented from doing so by smoke and flames coming from a nearby room or from below.

If you can't lean out of the window, lie close to the floor (where the air is cleaner) until you hear the fire brigade arrive.

If you have to escape before the fire brigade arrives, make a rope by knotting together sheets, tie it to a bed or other heavy piece of furniture, throw the end out of the window and climb down it.

If you can't make a rope and the situation becomes unbearable, drop cushions or bedding from the window to break your fall.

Go through the window feet first, lower yourself to the full extent of your arms and drop – into soft earth if possible.

If you are trapped in a room above first floor level, only drop to the ground as a last resort.

Clothing on fire

If your clothing catches fire, roll on the floor to extinguish the flames.

If someone else's clothing is on fire, lie them on the floor and roll them in blankets, rugs or a thick coat to extinguish the flames.

Anti-burglar quiz

	Yes/No
Do you have the locks changed when you move into a new home?	
Do you change locks if you lose your keys or have them stolen?	
Do you have a peephole or entryphone so that you can see or hear who is at your front door?	
Do you ask all unknown callers to identify themselves before you let them in?	
Do you know that the back of your house is as vulnerable to burglary as the front?	
Do you have all your external doors fitted with good quality rim or mortice locks, and bolts at top and bottom?	
Do you have external door hinges on the inside rather than the outside of your doors?	

Do you have all your windows fitted with anti-theft devices?
Do you keep unused doors locked at all times?
Do you always lock the garage door?
Do you lock the garden shed when you are not using it?
Do you lock up all ladders?
Do you keep house keys on you and not under the doormat or hanging on a string behind the letter-box?
Do you fasten all windows when you go out?
Do you lock all external doors and leave a light on or connected to a time switch, in a front room if you go out for the evening?
Do you tell the police when you are going to be away and who has the spare key?
Do you deposit valuables in the bank when you go away?
Do you ask a neighbour to keep an eye on the house when you are away?
Do you cancel milk and newspapers before going away?
Do you ask neighbours to mow your lawn when you go away in the summer?
Do you have photographs of all your valuable ornaments and jewellery?
Do you have a list of the serial numbers of your possessions? See *Serial numbers to keep* (page 120).
Do you have your alarm system regularly serviced?

Do you always deposit large
amounts of cash in a bank or
building society?

Do you lock any remaining
valuables away?

Do you remove all valuables from
your car before you leave it?

Do you always remove the ignition
key from your car when you leave
it?

Do you always lock boot, car
doors and fasten windows when
leaving your car?

Do you have an anti-theft device
in your car?

Do you always lock up your
bicycle?

*Did you answer 'Yes' to all (or most) of the
questions?*

Serial numbers to keep

Front door key

Car engine

Car chassis

Car licence plate

Car key

Petrol tank key

Motorbike chassis

Motorbike engine

Motorbike licence plate

Bicycle frame

Lawnmower

Vacuum cleaner

Washing machine

Tumble dryer

Dishwasher

Cooker

Fridge

Freezer

Food mixer

Television(s)

Radio(s)

Tape recorder(s)

Stereo system(s)

Camera(s)

Slide or film projector

Binoculars

Watches

Limited editions

Typewriter

Heater(s)

Hairdryer

These serial numbers could be helpful to the police if you are burgled or if you lose your car keys or need equipment serviced or repaired.

Why not insure against...

Your home collapsing. Make sure your home is adequately insured for the amount of money it would cost to rebuild it.

Your water tank overflowing.

Your home burning.

Your contents being vandalised. Insure possessions for their full value, but no more.

Your valuables being stolen.

Your car/boat/motorbike/bike getting damaged. If you own a car or a motorbike you are legally bound to take out motor insurance.

Your holiday being cancelled.

Your suitcase getting lost.

Being too ill to work.

Your life ending.

Your partner's life ending.

Paying for your child's education, in case you can't afford it later.

Having twins, for the second time.

Your mortgage not being paid.

Your antique furniture being broken when you move.

Your money and credit cards going astray.

Not earning enough money to be able to retire, if self-employed.

Any potential legal costs.

The judge dying and legal expenses being repeated.

Your pets getting ill.

Your vegetable garden being ruined by disease.

It raining on your charity garden party.

Although you may have to pay high premiums, you can insure against any eventuality.

Insuring your home

	Value for insurance
Carpets, rugs and floor coverings	£
Bedroom, bathroom and kitchen furniture	£
All tables, chairs, stools, suites, cabinets, sideboards, bookcases and lamps	£
Soft furnishings: curtains and their fittings, cushions, blinds	£
Televisions, radios and similar equipment	£
Household appliances: cooker, refrigerator, freezer, washing machine, vacuum cleaner, electrical goods, heaters, etc	£
Cooking utensils and provisions: cutlery, china, glass, food, drink and fuel	£
Valuables: gold and silver articles, jewellery, pictures, clocks, watches, cameras, ornaments and collections	£
Leisure: sports equipment, cycles, books, records, tapes, musical instruments and toys	£
Garden and garage equipment: furniture, lawnmower, ladders, tools, paints	£
Household linen: bedding, towels, table linen	£
Clothing	£
Attic contents: suitcases and their contents	£
Total	£

Add allowance for inflation if necessary, and add allowance for items to be bought during the year, approximately 5 per cent.

Transport

The cost of car ownership

Depreciation (the difference between the actual purchase price of your car and its resale value [when you sell it], divided by the years you owned it)	£
Interest (HP or, if the car is paid for, the interest you would have earned if your money had been invested elsewhere)	£
Vehicle licence	£
Insurance	£
Extras (radio, etc)	£
Petrol, oil, distilled water, etc	£
Services	£
Repairs (both parts and labour)	£
Tools	£
Cleaning equipment	£
Occasional car-washes	£
Membership of motoring clubs or organisations, breakdown services, etc	£
Maps	£
Tolls	£
Garage fees or parking permits	£
Parking meters and short-term garaging	£
Parking fines	£
Driving fines!	£
Total	£

Buying a used car

Check that you are paying the right price. See *Market research* (page 55).

Check *How to sell your car* (page 131), and realise that that is what you are up against.

Check that whoever is selling the car actually owns it, or has the right to sell it. Obtain written assurance from the vendor that the car is his.

Check whether or not there is an outstanding HP agreement.

Check the Vehicle Registration Document and old servicing bills.

Check the bodywork and underside for major rust defects. Use a small screwdriver to prod the underside gently – it should offer resistance.

Check the paintwork carefully. If it is patchy or bubbly rust may be starting underneath.

Check to see if there are any dents or ripples on the bodywork. Check for fibreglass by running a magnet over the car's surface – it if doesn't pull, there's no metal.

Check that the interior looks clean and tidy. Look under carpets for signs of water penetration or rust.

Check that the mileage reading seems reasonably accurate for the age of the car – look at the general condition of seats, pedal rubbers and carpets. (On average, cars are driven 10,000 miles per year.)

Check that the suspension is sound by pushing the car down firmly at each corner – the body should bounce once then return to a stable position.

Check hoses and electrics for signs of wear or neglect. Don't trust a dirty engine.

Check for leaks and rust on brake pipes.

Check that the tyres (including spare) have sufficient tread and are not unevenly worn, a sign of steering or suspension problems.

Check the exhaust system carefully for leaks

or loose mountings.

Check that all the lights work properly.

Check for oil or water leaks before and after your test drive.

Check the brakes by pumping the brake pedal several times when vehicle is stationary, before the test drive. If the pedal feels spongy at first and then hard it means that there is air in the hydraulic system. This may not be serious, but it's worth checking.

Check that you can change gear easily when test driving.

Check that the gears do not slip out.

Check that the steering is not slack or sloppy.

Check that the brakes stop the car effectively without your having to push the brake pedal to the floor.

Check brakes on a smooth road and notice whether the steering is pulling strongly to one side or another. The car should stay straight; if not, the brakes may be faulty.

Check for any other unusual handling characteristics or strange noises.

A quick, cheap way to put a car through its paces is to take it to a reputable garage and have an MOT test carried out. It will give you a good idea of the car's condition. Don't necessarily trust the MOT certificate the vendor shows you – his garage may not be as reputable!

MOT check list

Lighting equipment
Obligatory front
  lamps
Obligatory rear
  lamps
Obligatory
  headlamps
Headlamp aim

Stop lamps
Rear reflectors
Direction indicators

**Steering and
  suspension**
Steering controls
Steering mechanism

Power steering
Transmission shafts
  (forward only)
Stub axle assemblies
Wheel bearings
Suspension
Shock absorbers

Braking system
Service brake
  condition
Parking brake
  condition
Service brake
  efficiency
Parking brake
  efficiency
Service brake
  balance

Tyres and wheels
Tyre type
Tyre condition
Roadwheels

Seat belts
Security of mountings
Condition of belts
Operation

General items
Windscreen washers
Windscreen wipers
Horn
Condition of exhaust
  system
Effectiveness of
  silencer
Condition of vehicle
  structure

From the Check List for Vehicle Inspection,
published by Department of Transport.
Material reproduced with the permission of
the Controller of Her Majesty's Stationery
Office.

Economic motoring

Buy a manual rather than an automatic car.

Never ignore minor faults—they can only get worse.

Service your car as often as recommended by the manufacturer.

Check air and oil filters, spark plugs and correct engine timing.

Check front wheel alignment.

Check brakes are properly adjusted and not causing a drag on the wheels.

Think about buying radial tyres, if you haven't already. They last longer than cross-ply and save on petrol consumption.

Keep your tyres inflated 1–1.5kg (2–3

pounds) above the lowest recommended pressure.

Always use the grade of petrol suggested by the manufacturer.

Change oil when necessary, and don't buy inferior oil.

Don't carry unnecessary luggage in your car.

Avoid a roof rack unless essential.

Never warm up the engine before moving off – let the car warm up while moving.

Plan short journeys either one after the other or at the end of a long trip. When the engine is cold the car uses about twice as much petrol as it does when warm.

Use the choke for the minimum length of time possible. A well adjusted engine should be able to do without the choke within a mile.

Don't change speed quickly. Drive smoothly in top gear wherever possible, and keep the accelerator pressed as lightly as you can.

Make your top speed between 45 and 50 miles per hour.

Avoid fast starts, and stops.

Try and approach hills with enough momentum to carry you up the hill without having to change down a gear.

Don't use your gears as a brake.

Try to avoid driving in rush-hour traffic.

Switch off the engine if stuck in a traffic jam.

Sell your car!

No matter how much petrol you might save, never coast down hills with your car engine turned off; you may need to act quickly and be unable to do so.

Caring for your car

Weekly   Wash your car. (It makes it much quicker to clean.)

Get rid of all the rubbish that's accumulated inside during the week.

Monthly   Check the oil.

Check the water. (Open the radiator when the engine is cold.)

Check all tyre pressures when cold, including the spare.

Make sure tyres have sufficient tread. There should be 3mm of tread on the full circumference of the tyre, and on at least 75 per cent of the width.

See that there is enough distilled water in the battery. (You will probably use more distilled water in summer than in winter.)

Make sure all your lights work and replace any defective bulbs.

Check that there is water in your windscreen washer bottle.

Regularly   Service your car at the recommended intervals.

The moment you notice a fault, have it seen to.

Yearly   Renew road fund tax, resident's parking permits, insurance, etc.

Take MOT test if your car is over three years old.

In late autumn, make sure there is enough anti-freeze in the radiator. Consult the manufacturer's instructions to see if the car needs anti-freeze all year round.

Have your car serviced at least three days before you go on holiday, rather than the day before. More faults may show up than you anticipated.

How to sell your car

Find all the car's documents, repair bills, etc.

Think of all the wonderful things that apply to your car.

Read advertisements for similar cars and compare prices and descriptions.

Determine what is a fair price for your car, taking into consideration its age, mileage, condition, guarantee (if any).

Decide why you want to sell it. (If you don't have a good reason buyers are apt to get suspicious about its condition.)

Advertise in the local newspaper, and put a note in your car window and in your newsagent's window. Don't forget to include your phone number(s) and times to call.

Remove all rust patches, prepare the surface and retouch.

Touch up any other patches (if easy to do) and the chrome.

Don't have your car resprayed in order to sell it. (A respray may make the customer cautious.)

Clean the upholstery and vacuum the inside.

Wash the floor mats, or shampoo any loose carpets, and make sure they are dry before replacing them.

Clean out the boot, the glove compartment and any other storage areas.

Wipe the engine compartment with a damp rag to make it look cared for.

Wash the car thoroughly and keep it clean until you've sold it.

Check all the fluid levels to make sure the car will function properly in a test drive.

Check the tyres and adjust the pressures.

Make sure the lights work.

Check the tightness of locks, handles, window runners, etc, and make sure they don't rattle.

Don't spend money on repairing minor defects, such as a broken clock, as these faults may not bother the buyer.

Don't invest in major repairs before selling as you will never be able to recover the whole cost.

Remove your cassette player and anything else that you are not planning to sell.

Before a potential buyer arrives, go for a short drive to warm up the engine.

Be firm about the price initially, even if you are prepared to come down.

Be honest, but never apologetic, about your car.

Don't allow the customer to take the car for a test drive if the car is not fully insured.

If the buyer needs time to arrange finance, insist on a 5 or 10 per cent deposit.

Accept only cash, a banker's draft or cheque payment. Wait three days for a cheque to clear before handing over the car.

Read Hints on buying a used car (page 126), to know what the buyer is going to be looking for, and then correct the fault before it is noticed.

Don't forget that only in a very few cases is a car an investment. Always expect to lose money on a sale.

Motoring accessories

For everyone
Spare tyre (make sure it's roadworthy)
Aerosol can of tyre weld (for rush puncture repairs)
Jack
Set of spanners or an adjustable spanner
Pump
Tow rope
Warning triangle (for when you break down)
Set of jump leads
Battery charger (keep at home)
Empty petrol can
Fan-belt (make sure

you know what to do with it)
Spare bulbs (for all the lights)
Fuses (assorted)
Adhesive tape (for anything that drops off)
Oil (cheaper if you buy large quantities)
Distilled water
Window cleaner (plastic one side for scraping off ice, and rubber sponge on the other for dew)
Can of windscreen de-icer
Lubricant spray (for when locks jam or freeze)
Rags (for all messes)
Cleaning things (keep at home)
Torch (for night-time breakdowns)
Gloves (for would-be racing drivers)
Paper tissues (for checking oil and blowing noses)
Sunglasses (for sunny days and travelling incognito)
Glucose sweets (or others, for instant energy)
First aid kit (for emergencies)
Motoring organisation membership card and call box key
Maps (a set of good ones)

For enthusiasts
Workshop repair manual
Specialist tools for the car
Relevant size flathead and crosshead screwdrivers
Socket set and ratchet
2 pliers with different size and shape heads
Mallet with rubber or leather head
Spark plug socket
Feeler gauge (for adjusting spark plugs)

Car accident procedure

1. Keep calm.

2. Turn off your ignition.

3. Make sure any traffic can avoid you, so you don't cause another accident.

4. If you need to, get help by calling 999 or by asking a passing motorist to call emergency services.

5. If necessary, and if you know how to, apply first aid.

6. Write down the make, model and registration numbers of all vehicles involved.

7. Obtain the names and addresses of other drivers.

8. If the driver does not own the car he is driving, ask for the name and address of the person who does.

9. Do not discuss whose fault the accident was.

10. Ask for the names of all the drivers' insurance companies and their policy or certificate numbers. They are entitled to refuse to divulge this information; so may you.

11. Note any refusal to give information.

12. Write down details of any injuries.

13. Make a note of all damage to the vehicles.

14. Make a rough diagram showing how the accident occurred and include relevant information: time, date, weather, speed of vehicles involved, width of road, lighting, traffic lights, skid marks.

15. Take down names and addresses of any independent witnesses.

16. Note the names and numbers of policemen involved.

17. Inform your insurers as soon as possible if you wish to make a claim. Remember to report to your insurers any statements made at the scene of the accident by other parties.

Gallons to litres (and back)

1 gallon =	4.55 litres
2 gallons =	9.09 litres
3 gallons =	13.64 litres
4 gallons =	18.18 litres
5 gallons =	22.73 litres
6 gallons =	27.27 litres
7 gallons =	31.82 litres
8 gallons =	36.37 litres
9 gallons =	40.91 litres
10 gallons =	45.45 litres
15 gallons =	68.18 litres
20 gallons =	90.91 litres

1 litre =	0.22 gallon
5 litres =	1.1 gallons
10 litres =	2.2 gallons
15 litres =	3.3 gallons
20 litres =	4.4 gallons
25 litres =	5.5 gallons
30 litres =	6.6 gallons
50 litres =	11.0 gallons

Cyclist's tool kit

Universal or adjustable spanner	3 tyre levers
	Pliers/wire cutters
Puncture repair kit	Cycle oil
Pump	Cycle grease

If you don't look after your bike yourself, take it to a cycle shop every six months to be overhauled.

Bicycle safety

Both feet should be able to touch the ground simultaneously when you are sitting on your bike.

Wear fluorescent bands or a fluorescent waistcoat when bicycling, especially at night.

Get a helmet, but not a leather one.

Wear sunglasses or goggles rather than squinting.

Buy bicycle clips or tuck trousers into socks.

Don't wear a skirt in the wind—it may distract you (or others)!

Wrap fluorescent tape around the spokes and put reflectors on your pedals.

Make sure all your lights work when you go cycling at night.

Mount lights as high as possible and aim them at the level of motorists' eyes.

Get a loud horn, or practise shouting.

Ensure your brakes work effectively and your brake cables aren't frayed.

Check that your tyres have enough tread.

Make sure that tyres are properly pumped up.

Get chain guards.

Make sure that there are no sharp, protruding edges on your bike.

Plan your route before leaving home.

Keep your hands over or very near the brake levers.

Never ride two abreast.

Keep well clear of parked cars or vans in case one of them opens a door without seeing you.

Always check that it's clear behind you and signal before changing direction.

Be extra careful at road junctions.

Know your highway code.

Gardening

Basic gardening tools

Spade (of correct weight and length to suit you)
Fork (as spade, above)
Shovel
Rake
Dutch hoe
Draw hoe (for making seed drills)
Trowel
Dibber (or make your own by carving a broken fork or spade handle)
Garden hose
Watering can (a large galvanised iron one)
Lawn-mower (to suit your grass)
Edge clippers (if you have a lawn)
Hedge clippers (if you have a hedge)
Secateurs (for pruning)
Gardening gloves
Pruning saw
Wheelbarrow
Broom
Incinerator (or have a bonfire)

Planning your garden

See *So you're not green fingered* (page 140) for inspiration.

Study your neighbour's garden and note which of their plants are thriving.

Think about the type of garden you want and how you want to use it. Do you want it for entertaining, leisure, growing vegetables or drying the washing.

Consider how much time and money you are willing to spend on the garden. Remember, instant results cost money.

Decide what you want in your garden. Do you want a patio, terrace, children's play area, rock garden, pool or pergola?

Consider what you might need in your garden. Do you need a bicycle shed, greenhouse, summerhouse, garage, compost heap?

Think about the kind of garden that interests you. Do you like lawns, trees, shrubs, roses, herbaceous borders, fruit trees, vegetables, herbs?

Decide whether you would like a single-colour or multi-colour garden.

Draw up a plan of your proposed garden, to scale if possible.

Assess the features of your garden. Think about those you wish to keep and those you wish to dispose of.

Remember which direction your garden faces as the sun will affect the positioning of your plants.

Remember too, what type of soil you have as this will affect what plants you can grow.

Consider the needs of your children or pets.

Think about whether you want a formal garden based on geometric shapes or an informal one using flowing curves.

Consider planning your garden on an axis leading to a focal point, such as a statue, summerhouse or special tree.

Look to see if you can make use of any slopes in your garden, perhaps as a site for a rock garden or pool.

Consider using quarry stone, gravel or flagstones in place of a lawn.

If you want a lawn, remember to site paths carefully or people may take short cuts across the grass.

Discuss with neighbours the possibility of planting shrubs or hedges along common boundaries.

Don't start construction work or plant buying until you are certain of your overall plan.

Don't let your plan rule you or your garden. Relax and let nature and the weather make a few decisions too.

So you're not green fingered

Hire a gardener.

Turn your garden into a tennis court, a miniature golf course or a swimming pool!

Keep animals (chickens, rabbits, goats) and you won't have any space left for flowers.

Build a play area for your children.

Create a town house garden using paving stones and ornamental tubs.

Plant shrubs that need little (or no) attention.

Create a forest effect with silver birches and spring bulbs (snowdrops, crocuses, wood hyacinths, etc). Make random pathways and grow ivies and periwinkle to provide ground cover when the bulbs die down.

Build a pond with a paved surround, and fill it with water lilies.

Plant a lot of a few different hardy perennials (lupin, aster, pinks), but remember, you will have to wait a year for the results.

Let nature takes its course – just restrain the more exuberant growth, and encourage birds to visit by providing a bird table and bath.

Cultivate a lawn (hard work unless you leave edges rough and ignore daisies), and plant plenty of geraniums in baskets, window boxes, urns, etc.

Even if you have got green fingers, bear in mind that an average-sized garden (including a small vegetable plot) requires about 20 hours' work a week in the summer and about half that amount during the autumn.

Balcony vegetable garden

Aubergines
Cayenne peppers
Chinese cabbages
Courgettes
Cucumbers
Dwarf French beans
Lettuces

Marrows
Melons
Okra
Peppers
Potatoes
Tomatoes

All the above, apart from potatoes, can be grown from seed and then transferred to growbags. Potatoes can be grown in dustbins!

Ten easy indoor plants

1. Spider Plant: Prolific in a large pot, sever offspring and re-pot.

2. Sweetheart: Climbs and trails easily, but best in moist conditions.

3. Wandering Sailor: Tough and fast-growing, more colourful in the light. Trim off boring green shoots.

4. Castor Oil Plant: Big, bold and hardy. Keep moist, but watch out for greenfly.

5. Ivy: Grows vigorously, even in the shade. Climbing or trailing.

6. Swiss Cheese Plant: Large plant, with large leaves. Keep out of sun and tuck aerial roots back into the pot.

7. Parlour Palm: Compact jungle look. Grows slowly, just needs to be kept warm.

8. Aspidistra: Splendid long leaves. Reliable and can take both cool and shade.

9. Rubber Plant: An old robust favourite. If not over-watered it might grow to 3 metres (ten feet) high.

10. Yucca Plant: Suddenly very popular. Bright green leaves growing out of trunk. Sun lover.

Use herbs in...

Food seasoning (see *Basic* and *Cordon Bleu store cupboards,* pages 89 and 90).

Bouquet garni (fennel, marjoram, bay leaves, etc).

Herbal vinegars (tarragon, rosemary, marjoram, etc).

Herbal jellies (mint, tarragon, etc).

Herb butter (parsley, basil, oregano, etc).

Herbal teas (camomile, peppermint, rosehip, borage, etc).

Cat toys (catnip).

Moth repellent (santolina, wormwood, tansy, etc).

Pot-pourri (bay leaf, lavender, mint, lemon verbena, blue mallow, rose petals, etc).

Incense (sage, rosemary, southernwood, etc).

Herbal sachets (lavender, pot-pourri, etc).

Sleep pillows (peppermint, hops, marjoram, lavender, etc).

Bath fragrances (oil of lavender and rosemary, etc).

Herbal shampoos (rosemary, camomile, etc).

Dried flower and herb arrangements (fennel stalks, rosemary, etc).

Card decorations (instead of pressed flowers).

Easy indoor herbs

Borage
Chives
Fennel
Marjoram
Mint
Parsley
Rosemary (buy plant from nursery)
Sage
Sorrel
Tarragon (buy plant from nursery)
Thyme
Winter savory

Safety in the garden

Always keep gardening equipment in good condition. Put tools away after use.

Never leave tools lying on the grass.

Always store knives with blades covered, and shears with blades closed.

Always keep chemicals locked up, and never store them in soft drinks bottles.

Always follow instructions when using chemicals, and protect nose and eyes.

Always extinguish garden fires at night.

Never leave children unattended by a fire.

Never throw inflammable liquids onto a fire.

Always use a brightly coloured cable on your lawn-mower to avoid mowing over it.

Never use electric lawn-mowers when it is raining or when the grass is wet or leave them out in the rain.

Never pull an electric lawn-mower towards you, and never pick it up when it is on.

Never leave a mower unattended when the motor is running.

Always keep the electric cable over your shoulder and away from the blade when using power hedge-trimmers.

Always check garden swings, deckchairs, climbing frames, etc in the spring to see if fittings have corroded or rotted during the winter months.

Always teach children how to open and close deckchairs correctly.

Always supervise young children near water (pond, pool, etc) over 5cm (2 inches) deep.

Always make sure that children don't eat leaves, berries or flowers. (If they have, and appear to be suffering, take them to hospital with a sample of the plant.)

Always check fences to see that there are no protruding nails or splinters.

Pets

Should you get a pet?

	Yes/No
Will you be able to ensure the health and happiness of your pet after the initial novelty has worn off?	
Are you prepared to take on such a long-term commitment?	
Can you afford the financial burden of paying for its food, veterinary charges and kennel expenses when you go on holiday?	
Have you considered your life style and which is the right animal, if any, to suit it?	
Do your family (and landlord) agree?	
Have you got the time necessary to devote to a pet?	
Is your home large enough for a pet?	
Have you considered all the negative aspects of owning a pet?	

Do make sure you answer 'Yes' to all these questions before getting a pet.

Do you want a dog and...

8–16 years of devotion.

Walkies whenever it feels like it – even when you want to watch your favourite television programme.

Extortionate veterinary bills.

Exorbitant dog food costs – and the chore of carrying home an even heavier load of shopping from the supermarket.

Licence expense.

Kennel fees, when you've already got to pay for your holiday.

Personal problems: worms, fleas, illnesses, halitosis and pregnancy.

Hairs all over the carpet.

Saliva all over your suede skirt.

Damage done to other people's property, and even to other people!

Imploring whimpers every time you eat.

To be knocked to the ground whenever it wants to say hello.

Endless patience.

Or a cat and...

Hair balls in all the most unlikely places.

Missing goldfish and harrassed budgerigars.

Potential sexual problems.

Upholstery bills every six months.

Dead (or live) mice dropped at the bottom of your bed.

Delicious food constantly being rejected.

Chatting up neighbours so that you are free to go away on holiday.

Regular litters.

Hairs all over guests' clothes.

Refereeing cat fights.

Rescuing it from the tops of trees.

Rejection when you want to be affectionate, and having your legs stroked when you are cooking dinner.

Hefty vet's bills.

Compromises—for up to 15 years.

Cat and dog qualities

Dogs   Dogs keep you fit, in the nicest possible way.

Dogs are useful for hunting, tracking, herding, guarding, guiding and, of course, companionship.

Dogs are unbelievably loyal.

Dogs can be shouted at instead of your family, but do be nice to them afterwards.

Dogs let you meet other dog-lovers on walks.

Cats   Cats are excellent for catching vermin.

Cats can be left alone and are far less demanding than dogs or fellow human beings.

Cats are spotlessly clean.

Cats let you meet new people in the vet's waiting room.

Choosing your dog

Do you want a pedigree or a mongrel? (Pedigrees will be more expensive.)

Which breed to you want? (Remember how large your home is and what kind of temperament you would like your dog to possess.)

Do you want a dog or a bitch? (Bitches can be troublesome when on heat.)

Will you buy your dog from friends, from a registered breeder or a pet shop or through a local newspaper? (It is safer to buy your dog from a registered breeder because you should know what you are getting.)

Visit the litter to choose your dog when the puppies are between eight and ten weeks old.

Choose one with a temperament that is neither too aggressive nor too submissive.

Look for a puppy with clear, shining eyes.

Choose a plump puppy.

Look for one with thick, healthy fur which doesn't look dull.

Make sure the puppy's ears do not smell.

Check that the puppy doesn't have a cough.

Dog training principles

Once your dog is three months old, start regular training sessions.

Train for short spells once or twice a day.

If possible, one person only should train the dog, but make sure that the rest of the family support what is being done.

Teaching must be given kindly, patiently and with self-control on the part of the trainer; never lose your temper.

Have fun. Training should be enjoyable, both for dog and trainer.

First, train your dog to heel on a lead, then without a lead. Next, teach the basic commands 'sit' and 'here'.

Reward obedience with praise and, at first, with titbits, until the obedience becomes automatic. (Don't overfeed.)

Few dogs need more than a harsh word as punishment; don't hit your dog or it will become nervous and unreliable.

Remember that 'No' is a word your dog will learn almost immediately.

Dogs-when to call the vet

If it vomits persistently.

If it is constipated for a long time.

If it has skin trouble, such as sore or bare patches.

If it appears to have ear trouble: constant shaking of the head, scratching of the ear or the presence of a nasty smelling discharge.

If it has an irritation under its tail, such as abscesses or other swellings which might mean blocked anal glands.

If there is a possibility of worms, indicated by loss of weight, a dull coat and an occasional swollen tummy.

If it is listless, has dull watery eyes or a runny nose, which might mean a virus disease. (Call the vet immediately.)

If a puppy becomes dull and listless, or lacks appetite for more than a few hours.

If it has a sudden loss or increase in appetite.

If it is coughing, wheezing or sneezing.

If it appears to move painfully.

Questions and answers

1. Where can I get a cat?
Try most well-known animal rescue organisations.

2. How do I choose the best?
Don't worry, the cat chooses you!

3. How often should I feed my cat?
Usually twice a day.

4. What food is best?
Canned cat food contains a balanced diet with all the vitamins for good health. Extra titbits are welcome, of course. Never leave your cat without a bowl of water.

5. My cat keeps scratching, do you think he has fleas?

Probably. Try looking in his coat for tell-tale flea dirt. Use one of the dusting powders or sprays especially prepared for cats.

6. My cat seems unwell, what should I do?

See a vet. Never, never give your cat human medicines – you could kill him.

7. Is it cruel to 'doctor' my cat?

No. For a tom it is not an unkind cut. Toms often become more affectionate and stop unsociable habits around the house. It is cruel to let a 'queen' have litter after litter of unwanted kittens.

8. My cat is ruining the furniture, what shall I do?

Stop him when he starts to pluck the chairs, and provide him with a scratching post.

9. Should I put my cat out at night?

No, would you like to be put out in the cold?

10. Can my cat see in the dark?

No, but he can see in dim light which makes him a good night hunter.

11. I sometimes wonder if my cat dislikes noise?

Some dislike certain whistling sounds but some like music, and all cats can hear sounds inaudible to the human ear.

12. How do I stop my cat moulting over the furniture?

Groom him with a comb, every day if he has long hair.

List of twelve most frequently asked questions kindly compiled by Cat World Weekly *magazine.*

Other pets

Birds squawk, occasionally sing, eat a lot and make messes in their cages; they also need to be manicured!

Fish are extremely relaxing to watch, but don't offer much in the way of affection.

Rodents must be kept clean or they will inevitably smell; hamsters are antisocial as they only wake at night – ideal for insomniacs.

Rabbits live to breed, and eat; keep them well away from your vegetable patch, and other rabbits!

Tortoises are an extremely expensive hobby as they keep on vanishing – but, there again, they don't need a lot of attention!

Horses, donkeys, etc can be enjoyed just as much if you join a riding group—it's less work, friendlier and far cheaper!

Goats might almost be worth it for the milk and cheese!

Exotic animals can cause tremendous accommodation problems because of their growth rate, eg alligators. They may also be awkward to keep as they often like eating live food and thrive in an atmosphere similar to 'back home'!

Family

Questions and answers

1. Are any drugs safe in pregnancy?
Very few have been proved to do damage, but avoiding all drugs is much wiser. Consult your doctor about drugs at all times.

2. How can I get my child into modelling?
Most child model agencies are in the London area. Look in the Yellow Pages to see if there are any near you.

3. My child won't sleep at night, should I bring him into bed with me?
If he doesn't disturb you, let him come in. If he does, be firm; establish a routine and don't let him blackmail you out of it. It's dangerous to take a baby into your bed if you've taken sleeping tablets or had a few drinks.

4. How likely am I to have twins?
On average, twins occur once in every eighty pregnancies, but more often if there are already twins in the family.

5. What is 'structured' play?
It involves the active involvement of an adult who helps the child learn through play, rather than just leaving him to play freely.

6. I'm bad at story telling, so would it help to use story tapes?
Tapes should be an addition to, not a substitute for, the real thing. Don't worry, it's just a matter of practice.

7. At the birth, must I leave my wife if she has a caesarian?
Most likely yes if she has a general anaesthetic, but you are more likely to be allowed to stay if she has an epidural.

8. Should you bath a baby every day?
Not necessarily if his face, hands and bottom are kept scrupulously clean.

9. How can I try and prevent stretch marks?
Keep your skin well moisturised and supple. Use one of the proprietary creams or a good moisturiser over your breasts and stomach.

---

10. My baby is allergic to cow's milk—is there any alternative?
Many parents find goat's milk acceptable to allergic children; some opt for soya milk, though this is harder to obtain.

List of ten most frequently asked questions kindly compiled by Mother *magazine.*

Being pregnant

Read all you can about pregnancy, childbirth and babies.

Talk to your partner and friends about how you feel.

Decide with your doctor where you will have the baby.

Put a packet of dry biscuits by your bed for when you feel sick.

Don't smoke or drink.

Keep any pregnancy documentation with you all the time.

Take a urine sample with you every time you see the doctor.

Keep a check on how many weeks pregnant you are.

Eat healthy foods.

Remember to do ante-natal breathing and relaxation exercises during the last two months.

Take vitamin pills and iron tablets regularly, if necessary.

Unless absolutely necessary, do not take any drugs.

Once a day, put your feet up for half an hour.

Do take exercise, but don't overdo it.

Buy a pair of flat shoes.

Buy your largest maternity dress early on (you

won't feel like it later).

Don't forget to apply for Maternity Benefits (if employed) and Maternity Allowance and Grant from the government.

Buy basic baby things. See *Baby's layette* (page 156).

Pack your hospital suitcase 4 weeks before your baby is due. See *Hospital childbirth, pack . . .* (below).

Hospital childbirth, pack...

Several cotton nightdresses
Your sponge bag: soap, shampoo, face flannels
Bath towel
Slippers and dressing gown
Hairbrush and ribbons or bands (for long hair)
Eau de cologne or toilet water
Deodorant
Phone numbers of friends and relatives
Some change for the pay phone
Books to read
Writing paper and envelopes (and stamps)
Soft lavatory paper
Lip cream or vaseline (for dry lips)
A mineral water atomiser or a flannel (for use during labour)
Cotton nursing bra (to help prevent sore/cracked nipples) and disposable breast pads (if you want to breast feed)
Can of nipple spray or bottle of nipple lotion (if breast feeding)
Rubber ring to sit on (after episiotomy)
Sanitary belt and pads
Salt (for baths after episiotomy)
Throwaway pants

Also pack, but leave behind for someone to bring to the hospital later, a case with baby clothes and an outfit for you to go home in.

Top ten first names

The boys
James
William
Alexander
Thomas
Edward
John
Charles
David
Nicholas
Michael

And the girls
Elizabeth
Louise
Jane
Sarah
Charlotte
Victoria
Mary
Katherine
Alexandra
Lucy

As compiled by Margaret and Thomas Brown, taken from an analysis of names given to children whose birth or adoption was announced in The Times *in 1981.*

Baby's layette

4 cotton or fine woollen vests
6 stretch towelling suits or nightgowns
3 woollen cardigans
2 outdoor coats, mittens and bonnets, for winter babies
4 pairs bootees
A shawl or pram blanket
12 muslin squares to use for bibs, etc
6 pairs of plastic pants (at least)
24 nappies (terry towelling) and nappy liners (one way) or disposable nappies
6 nappy pins

Baby's room

Carry-cot and/or pram
Mattress
Waterproof sheet (for non-waterproof mattress)
Lined wicker crib or cradle (optional)
4 fitted cot sheets (minimum)
2 cellular cot blankets

2 flannelette cot blankets
Pillow (for babies over a year old)
Mobile (for baby to look at)
6 feeding bottles
6 teats
Sterilising container (plastic, with lid)
Sterilisation tablets or fluid (for bottles)
Bottle brush (nylon with a non-rust handle)
Low feeding chair with no arms and a padded seat (for you)
Baby bath (portable)
Safety mat (to prevent slipping)
2 bath towels (maybe one with a hood)
Plastic-backed towelling apron (for you)
3 baby wash cloths
Plastic changing mat
2 buckets with lids (for nappies)
Nappy sterilising solution
Toilet box/basket containing baby soap, shampoo, cream, vaseline, cotton wool, swabs, etc
Zinc and castor oil cream (for sore bottoms)
Baby wipes
Small nail scissors with blunt ends
Soft hair brush

Things children should do

Make their beds
Vacuum their rooms
Hang up their clothes
Put their dirty laundry in the laundry basket
Clean their shoes
Tidy their toys away

...and things they could do

Make cakes and biscuits
Shell peas
Lay the table
Wash up and dry
Load the dishwasher
Make you tea in the morning
Put out the milk bottles
Feed the animals
Clean out pets' cages
Sweep the path
Collect leaves in the garden
Beat cushions in the garden

Clean copper and
   silver
Polish the taps
Wash the bathroom
floor
Use the carpet
   sweeper
Polish furniture

These two lists are suitable for children aged five and over, depending on their skills.

Do supervise children, especially if they are washing the bathroom floor, and don't ever expect them to do anything as well as you can.

School Kit

Satchel or bag
Pencil case
Pen or magic
   markers
Pencils
Rubber
Ruler
Coloured pens
Notebooks
Basic geometry set
Tissues
Sandwich box
Sandwiches (make a
change from
   school dinners,
   and children can
   make their own)
Unbreakable
   drinking flask
Games uniform
   (shorts, T-shirts,
   etc)
Plimsolls
School uniform, if
   required
Plastic raincoat

What to tell the babysitter

Whether or not you'll be able to give them a lift home.

What time you'll return. (Be punctual or telephone if you are going to be late.)

Whether or not to open the front door if the doorbell rings.

Where the first aid kit is.

How to use the heating.

Where the nappies are kept and how to put them on.

Whether your baby will need teething jelly, and how much to rub on gums.

Where your children's toys are kept.

How the television works.

What your views are, if any, on your children watching TV.

What time the children should eat, if they haven't already.

Where the food is and how to prepare it.

Whether the animals need feeding.

What time your children should go to bed.

Whether they have a bedtime drink.

What they wash, brush, scrub, and how much help they need.

Whether they should be read to in bed or not.

What peculiarities they have (banana last thing at night, favourite cuddly toy, sleepwalking, etc).

Whether to leave their light on at night or not.

What your child's pet words for things are.

The telephone number of the place where you will be (even if it's the theatre, in which case give seat numbers).

Your doctor's telephone number.

The name, address and telephone number of a favourite neighbour in case you can't be reached.

Tell your babysitter what you want her (or him) to do; never assume a babysitter will do anything you haven't mentioned.

If your child is still a baby, make sure that your babysitter has had experience with babies and knows how to cope. Ask for references, and follow them up.

Keep your children safe

Alcohol: Keep your drinks cupboard locked up.

Animals: Make sure your children wash their hands before eating, especially if they have been playing with animals.

Bathrooms: Make sure your bathroom door can be opened from the outside, even when locked from inside.

Baths: Run children's baths with cold water first, then hot. Don't leave children alone in the bath.

Bicycles: Supervise children on bikes, scooters and tricycles.

Bonfires: Don't leave children alone near a bonfire, or let them play with fireworks unsupervised.

Cleaning materials: Keep cleaning materials locked up.

Cooker: Keep saucepan handles and kettle spouts turned inward on the burners.

Doors: Put safety locks and high handles on your front and back doors. Tie a bell to any door that you don't want your child to open so you can hear when they try.

Equipment: Constantly check climbing frames, slides and swings to see if they are safe.

Fires: Put a fixed fireguard in front of all fires. Never leave a child under 12 alone in a room with an unguarded fire.

Flexes: Tape the flexes of table lamps to the table legs so that lamps cannot be pulled off.

Garden: Always supervise children in the garden, especially if you have a pond, swimming pool or sand box.

Glass doors: Stick coloured tape at eye level on any sliding glass doors so that your child will be able to see if they are closed.

Kitchen: Never allow unaccompanied small children in the kitchen.

Knives: Never leave knives or other sharp utensils lying around.

Matches: Put matches, pins, glasses, ornaments and sharp objects out of children's reach.

Medicines: Always keep medicines and pills locked up. Do not leave them on your bedside table or in your handbag. Never let children help themselves to medicines.

Pillows: Don't let a child under one year old have a pillow in bed as it may suffocate him.

Plastic bags: Never let your child play with a plastic bag.

Road: Don't let children play in the road.

Stairs: Teach children how to climb up and down stairs as early as possible. Until they can, use a portable safety gate.

Tablecloths: Don't use tablecloths as they are tempting to pull.

Toys: Give children big rather than small toys to play with so that they cannot swallow them. For children under 6 months, make sure toys are plastic, non-toxic, washable, hygienic and have rounded edges. Check that cuddly toys have non-toxic fillings, firmly fixed eyes, no wires or spikes and no ribbon around their necks.

Windows: Never leave young children alone in a room with an open window, unless it has safety bars on it. Make sure windows in children's bedrooms and on landings have safety catches.

See also Safety *section.*

Keep your elders safe

Bathroom: Put a non-slip mat in their bath. Install a handrail near the bath and lavatory.

Burglars: See that their home is as burglar/vandal proof as possible. See *Anti-burglar quiz*, page 118.

Cold: Make sure that their home is warm and that they have enough thick clothes and blankets.

Fires: Check that all open fires have a guard round them.

Garden: Make sure that all paths and steps in the garden are well lit. Check that paving stones are level.

Kitchen: Always remove any chipped or broken crockery. Check that all saucepans have brightly coloured handles. Make sure they have a good can opener that is easy to use. Check that they have a plastic bowl in the kitchen sink.

Landing: Keep the landing lit all night.

Medicines: Never leave sleeping pills or other strong medications by their bedside. Never change their pills from one container to another. Label all medicines clearly. Make sure they can open child-proof medicine bottles.

Rugs: Attach nonslip backing to all rugs.

Stairs: Fix the stair carpet securely. Make sure that there is a handrail on the staircase.

See also Safety *section.*

Keeping in with in-laws

Never compete with them; remember you will never be able to do anything as well as they can.

Make sure they have got something to complain about.

Treat them as 'world authorities' on everything.

Always laugh at their jokes.

Send them regular photos of you, your partner and children (their grandchildren)!

Remember their birthdays, but not necessarily how old they are.

If you can, make their presents yourself: try knitting a scarf or making pâté or chocolate truffles.

Invite them round as often as you can stand it.

Make sure their gifts are prominently on display in your home.

Spring clean thoroughly before their visits.

Try cooking food you think they will like. Make jam, cakes, lemonade, etc.

Help with the washing up, but let them direct.

Ask them for ideas about how to look after their grandchildren, and tell them what a good job they did on your partner.

Ask to see baby photos of your husband/wife and be suitably enthusiastic!

If you do get on with your in-laws and none of the above apply to you, never forget how lucky you are.

Buying a present

How much do you want to spend?

Is this present for a special occasion?

Did they like what you gave them last time?

Have they recently hinted at something they'd like?

How could you make them feel special?

Would they prefer something you've made rather than bought?

Have they ever admired (covetted) anything of yours that you'd like to give them?

What are their hobbies or interests?

Have they just moved or finished decorating?

Could you get them something blue/red/green/brown to go in their new blue/red/green/brown room?

Do they live far away and will you have to post your gift?

What about a present related to their work?

Have they got any quirks like a bad back or insomnia that you could give them something for?

Could you give a present related to the characterisics of their Zodiac sign?

What about giving them something to encourage future plans?

Have you thought about giving two small presents rather than one large one?

Would they like a trip to the theatre or to the countryside?

Maybe they would like your help babysitting, cat-watching or even weed-digging. Why not give them some vouchers for future help?

Remember you are buying a present for someone else, not yourself. Use your imagination, and be thoughtful. If you decide to buy equipment, make sure you buy the make they like.

Once you've chosen with care, have fun wrapping up your parcel – even a plain white sheet of paper will do, so long as it looks exciting.

14 foolproof presents for men

1. Cologne or after-shave lotion (any that you like!)

2. A reclining chair (place it next to the television)

3. Clean his car (inside too)

4. A new record (which he will like, even if you don't)

5. A beautiful shirt (or any item of clothing you think it's about time he replaced)

6. A mini-computer

7. A barbecue grill (that way he will be happy to do the cooking when friends come round)

8. A squash racquet (to help keep him fit)

9. His favourite meal at home or out

10. Bottle of his special drink or a crate of wine or beer (depending on what he prefers)

11. A fabulous nightshirt or dressing gown

12. A stereo for his car

13. An electric drill or other tools (but only if he enjoys DIY)

14. A subscription to his favourite magazine

Guaranteed gifts for ladies

1. Her favourite fruit (out of season)

2. 2 theatre tickets

3. A cashmere or hand-knitted cardigan or jersey

4. Sexy underwear (if you think she will wear it)

5. A ring or fabulous piece of jewellery

6. Lots of pairs of different coloured tights or stockings

7. Anything that will make life in the kitchen shorter and/or more enjoyable

8. Anything to do with her hobby

9. Throw a dinner party for her, and hire cook and washer-upper (or do it yourself)

10. A gift voucher for a special shop

11. A bunch of flowers (possibly silk ones – they last)

12. A bottle of delicious liqueur

13. Do something around the house that she has wanted you (or someone) to do for ages

14. A bottle of her favourite perfume (or a new one to try that you find sexy)

Traditional children's gifts

0–1 year old
Cuddly animals
Squeaky toys
Mobiles
Building bricks (light ones)
Rattles
Something silver
Bath toys
Musical box
Shapes puzzles

1–3 years old
Plastic bat and ball
Wooden train or car
Toy robots
Rocking horse
Toys for a sandpit

Slide
Jigsaw puzzles (easy
  ones)
Large, soft balls
Plastic interlocking
  bricks
Sack of wooden
  building bricks
Bath toys
Bubble bath (non-
  toxic)
Paper and a set of
  wax crayons
Colourful beads
Tricycle
Pegboard and
  hammer

3–5 years old
Bubble-blowing kit
Wendy house
Dressing-up clothes
  (your old clothes)
Face paints
Clay modelling kit
Kaleidoscope
Model farm or zoo
Biscuit cutters
  (miniature cooking
  set)
Rubber stamp kit
Blackboard and
  chalk
Box filled with
  pencils, blunt-
  ended scissors,
  crayons, coloured
  paper, etc

5–8 years old
Roller skates
Labyrinth game
Table football
Printing kit
Junior word games
Engineering set
Pogo stick
Junior typewriter
Bicycle with training
  wheels

Small loom and
  coloured wool
Magic set
Skipping rope
Dominoes
Portable record
  player

8–12 years old
Electronic games
Tennis racquet (and
  lessons)
Personalised mug
Walkie-talkie
Pencil case (filled
  with silly things)
Sled
Board games
Toy theatre (let them
  make the puppets)
Pair of stilts
Kite
Posters
Diary
Subscription to a
  favourite magazine
Torch
Camera
Candle-making kit
Cooking utensils
Globe

Teenagers
Dart board
Sleeping bag and
  tent
Calculator
Simple make-up kit
Jewellery
Backgammon
Radio alarm
Sewing machine
Jeans, T-shirts or
  shoes
Trip to a fast-food
  restaurant (let them
  go alone)
Diary with padlock
Television
Driving lessons

Health

Prevention is better...

An orange a day keeps the doctor away.

Stop smoking now, or cut down considerably. For how to stop, see *No more smoking* (below).

Don't drink alcohol to excess, although an occasional drink is good for you.

Eat plenty of fibre. Bran is best, but green vegetables, cereals and fruit are good too.

Take strenuous exercise twice a week, and that's more than chasing after a bus. (Over 35s, please consult your doctor before you start doing this.)

Eat vegetable fat in preference to animal fat.

Diet, if you are overweight. See *Slimmers' hints* (page 171).

Get enough sleep. Take plenty of rest and give yourself enough time to relax.

Eat small, balanced meals at regular intervals during the day rather than one large one at night.

No more smoking

Analyse the number of cigarettes you enjoy and recognise how many you don't.

Make a list of the reasons why you want to stop, and re-read it.

Tell everyone you know that you are going to stop.

Look forward to being healthy, rich and sweet-smelling.

Stop smoking suddenly and completely. This is better than cutting down gradually.

When you are offered a cigarette, don't say you've given up – say you don't smoke.

Put the money you would have spent on

cigarettes in a piggy bank. You will soon be disgusted at how much smoking costs you.

Keep a packet of cigarettes on you, so you know you could smoke if you really wanted to.

Change your habits. Have orange juice after your meal instead of coffee or tea.

Start running for buses, cycling or playing squash. Notice how much better you feel.

Avoid pubs for a while and other situations where lots of people are smoking.

Remove all cigarette butts from your home and car.

Keep your hands busy, especially when watching television. Darn everyone's socks, dig out your old worry beads or play with a pencil.

If you get tense, do some deep breathing exercises for a minute or two. Breathe all the way in, hold your breath for a few seconds, then breathe all the way out. Stretch your lungs.

When you want a cigarette, have a carrot or some chewing gum instead. (Try nicotine flavour – it's disgusting.)

At the end of the day, relax in a bath or have a drink. (Don't overdo it.)

Don't worry about not smoking for ever, just worry about not smoking today.

Remember, every day it will become easier.

Try not to eat too much as a substitute for cigarettes. Giving up food isn't much fun either.

If you are finding it extremely difficult to give up, visit a smoking withdrawal clinic. Get details from your local Area Health Authority.

Or try hypnosis . . .

Stop biting your nails

Analyse why and when you bite your nails and devise an alternative occupation.

Become jealous of friends with fabulous long nails.

Have false nails fitted for a while and then get out of the habit – you can't bite them!

Get your stubbly nails manicured to give you a good start, and buy a manicure set.

Coat your nails with bitter aloes or bright red nail varnish.

Start wearing rings.

Learn how to use a nail file.

Watch someone else biting – it's a real turn-off.

If it's the only bad habit you've got – keep biting!

Or ... try your toe nails. They don't show!

Slimmers' hints

Choose a diet you like and believe in and keep to it.

Remember your goal, even when everyone starts telling you how great you look.

Try to convince yourself that you don't like cream cakes, or chocolate bars.

Carry on boosting your morale by continually reading about dieting and exercise.

Imagine yourself as looking really good, and thin, and you'll soon start acting in ways that will make it happen.

Relax before you start to eat so that you eat slowly, enjoy it more and need less.

Be formal about meals, lay the table and eat

them sitting down.

The moment food is put on your plate (in a restaurant, with friends, etc), cut the portion in half and eat only one half.

Try and avoid situations in which you would love to be eating, and avoid being near foods you can't resist.

Exercise a lot – dieting gets easier as you get thinner.

Stick pictures of enviably thin bodies all round your kitchen – and keep moving them about so that you don't ignore them.

Eat only when you're hungry and stop the moment you're satisfied.

Learn how to say 'No'.

Make sure you reward yourself for the things you accomplish, but never with food.

Experiment in the kitchen with food that is good for you. Grow to love vegetables and fruit.

Never eat just before going to bed.

Never skip meals.

Don't feel you have to finish what is on your plate. Your body is not a dustbin.

Throw out any leftovers.

Put everything you eat on a plate so that you can see the amount. Don't put it straight from the fridge into your mouth.

When you're alone and feeling hungry, pretend your lover is with you and control yourself accordingly.

Use small plates.

Learn how to enjoy things without food having to be involved.

Try dieting with a friend.

Calorie counting

	Average portion	Calories
Avoid these		
Bacon, streaky	50g (2oz)	300
Beans, baked	150g (5oz)	130
Beef, corned	75g (3oz)	200
Beer	250ml ($\frac{1}{2}$ pint)	90
Cake, iced, 1 slice	50g (2oz)	210
Cheese, cream	25g (1oz)	145
Chocolate, milk/plain	50g (2oz)	320
Coffee, milk and sugar	1 cup	85
Cornflakes	50g (2oz)	204
Cream, thick	25ml (1fl oz)	100
Doughnut	50g (2oz)	195
Flour	25g (1oz)	100
Ham, fat	100g (4oz)	375
Lamb, fat	100g (4oz)	375
Mayonnaise	25g (1oz)	110
Peanuts	50g (2oz)	335
Pork, fat	100g (4oz)	450
Potatoes, chipped	100g (4oz)	270
Raisins	50g (2oz)	140
Rice, uncooked	25g (1oz)	90
Sardines	50g (2oz)	175
Semolina, uncooked	50g (2oz)	195
Spaghetti, uncooked	50g (2oz)	190
Spirits (brandy, gin, etc)	50g (2oz)	125
Sugar	15g ($\frac{1}{2}$oz)	50
Syrup	25g (1oz)	80

	Average portion	Calories
Think before eating these Apricots, canned	120g (4oz)	60
Banana, one		92
Beans, butter	25g (1oz)	25
Beef, roast	65g (2½oz)	160
Biscuits plain	25g (1oz)	160
Bread	1 slice	75
Butter	15g (½oz)	115
Cheese, Cheddar	75g (3oz)	360
Cocoa, ½ milk	1 cup	110
Fruit juices	150g (5oz)	75
Haddock	100g (4oz)	108
Herring	100g (4oz)	217
Honey	25g (1oz)	80
Ice cream, vanilla	50g (2oz)	115
Jam	15g (½oz)	35
Jelly	100g (4oz)	85
Margarine	15g (½oz)	130
Marmalade	15g (½oz)	35
Milk, fresh	250ml (½pt)	190
Mineral waters, artificial	1 glass	100
Peaches/pears, canned	100g (4oz)	90
Peas, canned	75g (3oz)	72
Pineapple, canned	100g (4oz)	72
Pork, lean	75g (3oz)	270
Potatoes, boiled	2	120
Salmon, fresh/canned	75g (3oz)	120
Sausages, beef	100g (4oz)	289
Sausages, pork	100g (4oz)	372
Soup, thick	225g (8oz)	120
Tea, milk, sugar	1 cup	75
Wines, average	100g (4oz)	85

		Average portion	Calories
Eat these	Apple	1	65
	Bacon, lean	50g (2oz)	175
	Beans, French/ runner	50g (2oz)	4
	Beetroot	50g (2oz)	26
	Brussels sprouts	100g (4oz)	20
	Cabbage/cauliflower	100g (4oz)	10
	Carrots	75g (3oz)	15
	Celery	75g (3oz)	9
	Cherries, fresh	100g (4oz)	48
	Chicken	100g (4oz)	165
	Cod fillets	150g (5oz)	115
	Coffee with milk	1 cup	30
	Cucumber	50g (2oz)	5
	Eggs, boiled	1	80
	Grapefruit	175g (6oz)	20
	Grapes	100g (4oz)	78
	Ham, lean	75g (3oz)	185
	Lamb, lean	100g (4oz)	230
	Lettuce	90g (3½oz)	10
	Liver	100g (4oz)	160
	Marrow	100g (4oz)	10
	Mushrooms	50g (2oz)	4
	Onions	100g (4oz)	16
	Orange	1	40
	Parsnips/turnips	100g (4oz)	35
	Peaches, fresh	100g (4oz)	60
	Pear, fresh	100g (4oz)	60
	Pineapples, fresh	175g (6oz)	65
	Plaice, steamed	100g (4oz)	104
	Plums, fresh	75g (3oz)	30
	Radishes	25g (1oz)	2
	Raspberries, fresh	100g (4oz)	25
	Rhubarb	100g (4oz)	5

	Average portion	Calories
Shrimps	50g (2oz)	60
Sole, steamed	100g (4oz)	95
Soup, thin	100g (4oz)	20
Strawberries	175g (6oz)	42
Tea, milk, no sugar	1 cup	20
Tomatoes, fresh	75g (3oz)	12
Turkey	100g (4oz)	185
Veal	75g (3oz)	198

Avoid fried food altogether.

Work out your total daily calorie allowance and stick to it.

Follow the 'metric' diet and you'll lose more weight!

When you're ill

Colds If you can, go to bed and keep warm.

Drink plenty of fluids. Eat well if you feel like it.

Take vitamin C tablets the moment the cold appears.

If you have a headache or sore throat, take 2 soluble aspirins in cold water every 4 hours to relieve the pain and reduce the fever.

Coughs If you smoke, stop.

Take cough medicines or sweets if they help.

Drink lots of hot lemon juice with water and honey.

Flu or fever Go to bed and keep warm.

Drink plenty of fluids.

Take 2 soluble aspirins every 4 hours to make you feel better.

Sore throats Stop smoking.

Drink a lot of hot drinks, especially hot lemon and honey, as above.

Take 2 soluble aspirins every 4 hours, as above.

Try sucking some antiseptic throat lozenges from the chemist.

Gargle with a suitable antiseptic liquid.

Mild stomach pains If you think it may be indigestion, lie down with a light hot water bottle on your stomach.

Take an indigestion tablet if the pain does not pass.

Vomiting Remove yourself from the cause of your nausea, if possible.

Lie flat and keep warm.

Wait a few hours and try drinking a little water.

Eat carefully for the rest of the day and the next day.

Diarrhoea If you know the cause then you'll probably be better tomorrow. Until then, drink lots of fluids and don't eat unless you feel like it.

Take a tablespoon of kaolin morphine mixture if you can't manage to get to the lavatory.

Acute vomiting or diarrhoea Drink several glassfuls of this concoction: 250ml ($\frac{1}{2}$ pint) water with a tablespoon of sugar and a teaspoon of salt. It works.

Eat nothing for the next 24 hours.

Constipation Eat a balanced diet, including plenty of fruit, raw vegetables, wholemeal bread and bran. Go to the lavatory if you feel like it.

Don't take laxatives until you've tried eating properly for a few weeks.

Headaches Try and work out why you've got the headache.

To release tension, try taking deep breaths of fresh air or massaging your neck or temples.

If you're feeling hungry have a light meal and a cup of coffee.

Otherwise, lie down in peace and quiet and take a paracetamol tablet.

Rashes   Rashes may be due to heat or to an allergy. Think whether you've changed soap, cosmetics or washing detergent recently and change back.

If any of the problems mentioned above are persistent, recurrent or worsening, don't hesitate to consult your doctor.

You should call the doctor...

If you feel really ill.

If you've been feeling mildly ill for some time and don't seem to be improving.

If any of the 'minor illnesses' on the previous list seem to be getting worse.

If you are continually gaining or losing weight.

If you never seem to be hungry.

If you feel tired all the time, even though you are sleeping a lot.

If you have a persistent headache.

If it hurts when you pass water and you find you want to do so frequently.

If you have an unusual and persistent cough not associated with a cold, or one producing green sputum.

If you have an unusual vaginal or penile discharge.

If you have an unexplained rash that has lasted for longer than a week.

If you have unexplained bleeding from any part of your body.

If you have continued or recurrent pain anywhere in your body.

If you have sores that don't heal.

If you have boils round your nose or upper lip.

If there's a change in your moles or birth-marks.

If you think you may be suffering from an infectious illness.

If you have an abdominal pain which lasts for longer than 6 or 8 hours or gets worse, especially if accompanied by vomiting and loss of appetite.

If you have a gripping central chest pain, especially if you are over 35.

If you are having serious difficulty in breathing.

If unconsciousness occurs for any reason, especially after injury.

If you have continuous backache.

If you have severe bleeding.

If you have swellings or lumps anywhere on your body.

If you have a change of bowel habit.

If you have excessive thirst and passing of water.

If you have visual problems such as double or blurred vision.

If you are giddy or weak and falling over a lot.

If your hearing is getting worse.

If you are feeling severely anxious or depressed.

If you have acute joint pain or stiffness or swelling.

If you have painful feet which are affecting your mobility (especially if you are over 60).

Always consult your doctor first. Do not go to a hospital Casualty Department unless it is an obvious emergency or accident.

Basic medicine cupboard

Thermometer
Sterile cotton balls
Sterile gauze pads
Antiseptic (liquid and
  cream)
Scissors
Gauze bandages
  (narrow and wide)
Safety pins
Roll of adhesive tape
  (for securing
  bandages)
Paraffin gauze (for
  cuts)
Crêpe or elastic
  bandages (for
  sprains)
Surgical tweezers
Packet of needles
  (for splinters)
Assorted plasters
Skin closure strips
  (for small cuts)
Eye wash and eye
  cap
Insect repellent
Petroleum jelly

Soluble aspirin or
  paracetamol
Cough syrups (a
  simple linctus to
  soothe cough and
  an expectorant)
Throat pastilles and
  antiseptic
  lozenges
Measuring cup or
  spoon
Antacid (for stomach
  aches and
  heartburn)
Calamine lotion
Mild steroid cream
  (for bites and
  stings)
Antifungal powder or
  cream (for athlete's
  foot)
Mild laxative
An antidiarrhoeal
  preparation
Travel sickness pills
Ear drops

Medicine cupboard check

Store drugs in a small, lockable cabinet outside your bathroom – they should be kept cool and dry.

Be sure that your children cannot open the cabinet – move it if they can, or make sure the lock works.

Make sure the cabinet is well lit – so that you do not take the wrong drug by mistake.

Organise your cabinet so that everything is easy to find.

Write the telephone number of your doctor

and local hospital on a card and stick it on the door of the cabinet.

Get rid of all over-the-counter drugs that have passed their expiration date or are over a year old.

Destroy anything that has lost its label.

Throw all old medicines down the lavatory – don't put them into the dustbin or on the fire.

Throw away all ointments and creams that have hardened or separated.

Get rid of all liquids that have become cloudy or discoloured, or have formed a sludge at the bottom of the container.

Remove tablets that have crumbled, capsules that have broken or melted and tinctures from which alcohol has evaporated.

Keep all dangerous drugs in childproof containers.

Mark each drug you are keeping with the date of purchase, the name of the drug and the reason why it was prescribed.

From now on, label new drugs automatically.

Getting rid of hiccups

Eat a large spoonful of granulated sugar.

Drink a glass of water from the wrong side of the glass (the side furthest from you).

Hold your breath and swallow quickly as often as possible.

Eat a small piece of ice.

Drink directly from the tap rather than from a glass.

Take deep regular breaths through your nose for a few minutes, or until the hiccups go.

Gargle with plain hot or cold water for a minute or two.

Cover your mouth and nose with a paper bag and inhale and exhale into it for a few minutes. (The accumulation of carbon dioxide in the bag sometimes stops the spasms.)

Take a deep breath and hold it for as long as possible.

Stand with your back against the wall and ask a friend to press hard with their fist right at the centre of your upper abdomen between the margins of your rib cage. Stay like this for a few minutes.

If your hiccup attack persists for an hour or more, you should consult your doctor.

Presents for invalids

Selection of their favourite magazines

Foreign language cassette course

Some 'cordon bleu' dinners

A book of cartoons (unless they have stitches)

Knitting needles and wool, and a pattern

Some pot pourri for sweet-smelling rooms

A silver spoon to help the medicine go down

A bell to ring when they are being demanding

A wastepaper basket for endless tissues

A kaleidoscope, for when the ward starts to look boring

A picture or poster of a pleasing landscape

A bowl of chicken soup (Jewish penicillin)

A bed tray

A good detective novel, or a hospital romance

Writing paper and stamps

Book of crossword puzzles

Plasticine, so they can sculpt the nurses

Clothes

Hints on dressing well

Know what suits you.

Look after your clothes.

Buy clothes in one or two colours and black and white.

Use accessories to change outfits.

Avoid extremes of fashion.

Clothes buying quiz

Yes/No

Can you afford it?

Does it suit you?

Have you tried it on?

Does it look good from all angles?

Does it fit properly?

Does it go with anything else in your wardrobe?

Does the colour match the specific item you want to wear it with?

Will you be able to wear it often?

Is it easy/cheap to clean?

Is it well made?

Could you lengthen it if you wanted to?

Are the buttons firmly sewn on?

Are they all there?

	Yes/No
Are there any spare buttons?	
Is the material fault-free?	
Is it clean?	
Do you like it?	
Do you really need it?	
Can you return it later if you decide you don't want it?	
Would your money be refunded?	

Did you answer 'Yes' to at least 75 per cent of the above questions?

Don't buy anything that is too small, even if you are on a diet and hope to slip into it easily within a few weeks.

Remember, if you can find what you want, it is usually cheaper to buy clothes off-season.

Women's clothes sizes

Size	Bust/hip	Waist
8	76/81cm (30/32″)	58cm (22″)
10	81/86cm (32/34″)	61cm (24″)
12	86/91cm (34/36″)	66cm (26″)
14	91/97cm (36/38″)	71cm (28″)
16	97/102cm (38/40″)	76cm (30″)
18	102/107cm (40/42″)	81cm (32″)
20	107/112cm (42/44″)	86cm (34″)
22	112/117cm (44/46″)	91cm (36″)
24	117/122cm (46/48″)	97cm (38″)
—	—	102cm (40″)
—	—	107cm (42″)

Men's clothes sizes

Collar	Chest	Waist
36cm (14″)	81cm (32″)	71cm (28″)
38cm (15″)	84cm (33″)	76cm (30″)
39/40cm (15½″)	86cm (34″)	81cm (32″)
41cm (16″)	91cm (36″)	86cm (34″)
42cm (16½″)	97cm (38″)	91cm (36″)
43cm (17″)	102cm (40″)	97cm (38″)
44cm (17½″)	107cm (42″)	102cm (40″)
46cm (18″)	112cm (44″)	107cm (42″)
—	117cm (46″)	112cm (44″)
—	122cm (48″)	117cm (46″)
—	127cm (50″)	122cm (48″)

Clothes care symbols

Washing		Ironing	
Hand wash only		Hot iron (210°C) – use for cotton, linen and viscose	
Do not wash		Warm iron (160°C) – use for polyester mixtures and wool	
Bleaching		Cool iron (120°C) – use for acrylic, nylon, acetate, triacetate and polyester	
Chlorine bleach may be used			

Do not iron	⊠	Drying	☐
Dry clean	◯	Tumble drying beneficial	⊡
May be dry cleaned	Ⓟ		
Do not dry clean	⊗	Do not tumble dry	⊠

Washing symbols

1 / 95° White cottons and linens without special finishes (towels, sheets, napkins, vests, handkerchiefs).

2 / 60° Cottons, linens or viscose articles without special finishes (coloured tea-towels, tablecloths, pillowcases).

3 / 60° White nylon and white polyester/cotton mixtures (school shirts, underwear, girls' socks).

4 / 50° Coloured nylon; polyester; cotton and viscose articles with special finishes; acrylic/cotton mixtures; coloured cotton/polyester mixtures (printed sheets, undies, girls' dresses, stretch covers, polyester net curtains).

5 / 40° Cotton, linen or viscose articles, colour fast at 40°C but not at 60°C (loose covers, curtains).

6 / 40° Acrylics; acetate and triacetate, including mixtures with wool; polyester/wool blends (cot blankets, skirts, sweaters, acetate curtains).

7 / 40° Wool and wool mixtures with cotton or viscose; silk (blankets, silk dresses and shirts, jumpers).

Silk and printed acetate fabrics with colours not fast at 40°C (dresses and blouses unlikely to be UK produced).

Most of your wash will probably fit into categories 1, 2 and 4.

The art of ironing

Avoid it wherever possible!

Ensure that the flex comes from behind you and goes to your working side.

Use a padded cover on your ironing board.

Make sure clothes are at the right stage of dampness (almost dry). Clothes, apart from linen, can be dry if you have a steam iron.

If you haven't got a steam iron, use spray water to dampen clothes.

Use distilled water in your steam iron and empty it after use. (Tap water builds up scale.)

Check with attached care labels to know what heat setting to use.

Start ironing items that need a cool iron. (Irons take about five minutes to adjust from one heat setting to the other and you might get impatient!)

If you think the iron may be too hot, always test it on a seam or hem.

Pull clothes into shape and lay them flat on the ironing board.

Always iron into gathers.

When ironing circular table cloths, mats, etc, iron from the outside and work towards the centre.

Pull pleats into shape and iron on top.

Iron dark-coloured fabrics, silk and fabrics which glaze badly on the wrong side, or under a damp cloth.

Start by ironing double parts (eg collars) on the wrong side, then iron the right side.

Iron fiddly bits such as frills, yolks, cuffs, collars first, then iron the large surfaces.

Use spray starch to help shirts and blouses look brand new.

Beware of nylon zips being fitted into cotton clothes which need to be ironed with a hot iron – the zips may melt.

If, while ironing, the iron refuses to glide over the material and starts sticking, let it cool down.

Never walk out of a room leaving the iron on.

Never rest the iron with the sole plate down, rest it on its heel.

After ironing, leave clothes to air and become bone dry before wearing them or putting them away.

Never iron dirty clothes. If you really have to, brush them thoroughly first.

Ironing fabrics

Acrylics and acrylic/wool blends: Iron dry on the wrong side with a cool to warm setting; do not use a steam iron.

Angora: Do not iron.

Cotton: Iron when damp (or use a steam iron) with a hot setting.

Drip-dry cottons: If you must iron them, use a cool setting.

Embroidery: Pad the ironing board with a towel covered with a tea towel and place the embroidery face down on it. Put a damp cloth (either cotton or linen) over the top and iron quickly with a hot iron.

Knits: Steam iron or iron slightly damp with a warm iron on either side; be careful not to stretch out of shape.

Linen: Iron when damp (even if using a steam iron) with a very hot setting. Iron on wrong side for matt finish, on right side for a shiny finish.

Man-made fibres: Use a cool iron on the wrong side. Be careful that buttons and zips don't melt.

Mixed fibres: Set the iron for the fibre needing the coolest temperature. Check that the fabric is not marked 'Non-iron'.

Mohair: Do not iron.

Silk: Use a warm iron on the wrong side when silk is very damp. Always test temperature on seam or hem first.

Suits or coats (wool): Iron under damp cloth with medium hot iron. Beat steam out of fabric so that it won't mark or shrink.

Velvet: Iron face down on a velvet board, if possible. If not, cover ironing board with a thick towel and iron lightly on wrong side with a warm iron.

Sewing Kit

Assorted needles
Pins
Sewing threads
Large reels of black
    and white tacking
    cotton
Multi-coloured
    sewing plait
Reel of heavy-weight
    button thread
Thimble
Safety pins, and a
    magnet for
    collecting them
Pin cushion,
    preferably one you
    can wear on your
    wrist
Small, sharp pair of
    scissors

Cutting shears
Pinking shears
Seam ripper
Tape measure, with
    both metric and
    imperial measures
Iron-on mending
    patches
Darning mushroom
Darning wools
Buttons you've
    collected
Press-studs, hooks
    and eyes
Binding, tapes,
    elastic
Ribbons
Tailor's chalk
Sewing machine plus
    attachments

Stain removal Kit

Absorbent pads (soft white clothes, paper tissues)
Absorbent powders (talcum powder, French chalk)
Soda syphon
Clothes brush
Blotting paper
Dry-cleaner – aerosol, liquid or paste
Enzyme detergent
Pre-wash aerosol
Glycerine
Eucalyptus oil
Washing soda
Bicarbonate of soda
Borax
Chlorine bleach
White spirit/ turpentine
Lighter fuel
Acetone
Non-oily nail varnish remover
Methylated spirit

Be careful when storing and using cleaning agents. Some are highly inflammable and poisonous.

Always follow instructions, if given.

Always test the cleaning agent first in an inconspicuous place.

Never use dry cleaning fluids near a naked flame, or smoke while using them.

See Removing stains (fabrics), *page 192.*

Stain removal hints

Always act fast. Treat all stains immediately.

Always blot area dry or remove surface deposit first.

Never use hot water – it will set the stain.

Always immediately sprinkle grease stains with absorbent powder, cover fruit/wine/ beetroot stains with salt and rinse other stains with cold water.

Always follow manufacturer's fabric cleaning instructions when available.

Always read instructions on cleaning agents' containers first.

Always test cleaning agents in an inconspicuous place first.

Always use a weak solution of a cleaning agent several times rather than a strong solution once.

Always place an absorbent pad behind the stained fabric, keeping the wrong side of the fabric on top (unless it's a carpet or a fitted chair cover).

Always work from the outside of the stain in, to avoid leaving rings.

Always complete any treatment by rinsing thoroughly in cold water, and, if chemicals have been used, wash article in soapy water before rinsing.

Always dry the fabric quickly with a hair-dryer to prevent a ring being left.

Never soak wool, silk, non colour fast or flameproof fabrics.

Never use absorbent powders on carpets, they're difficult to remove.

Always consult professionals if you don't know what the stain is, or if it persists.

Removing stains (fabrics)

Alcohol: Sponge with detergent solution.

Baked beans/beetroot: Soak in enzyme detergent solution.

Ballpoint ink: Use methylated spirit.

Blood: Rub with cold water and salt. If necessary, use enzyme detergent solution.

Butter: Remove deposit and cover stain with absorbent powder, then use dry-cleaner.

Candle wax: Scrape off wax, place blotting paper above and below fabric and iron using warm iron.

Chewing gum: Either chill with an ice cube in a polythene-bag (to avoid wetting fabric) and scrape off, or use dry-cleaner.

Chocolate: Remove deposit, then use enzyme detergent solution.

Coffee and tea: Sponge with borax solution or use glycerine solution.

Cosmetics: Use glycerine or dry-cleaner.

Crayon: Use dry-cleaner or lighter fuel.

Cream: Soak or sponge with enzyme detergent or borax solution, then use dry-cleaner.

Dog or cat messes/vomit: Remove deposit, then use enzyme detergent or borax solution.

Egg: Remove deposit, then use cold salt water then enzyme detergent solution or dry-cleaner.

Fruit juices: Cover with salt or soak in cold salt water. Use mild bleach solution on white fabrics.

Grass: Use eucalyptus oil or glycerine or methylated spirit.

Gravy: Remove deposit, then use cold water and then dry-cleaner.

Ice cream/ice lolly: See Cream.

Jam: Remove deposit, then sponge with liquid or enzyme detergent solution.

Lead pencil: Use an india rubber, then dry-cleaner or methylated spirit.

Mildew: Moisten with lemon juice and salt, then dry in the sun. If necessary, use peroxide solution.

Milk: Use cold water, then wash as usual. Use dry-cleaner if necessary.

Nail varnish: Remove deposit, then use non-oily nail varnish remover or amyl acetate.

Oil: Cover stain with absorbent powder, then use dry-cleaner.

Paint (oil-based): Remove deposit, then use cold water immediately.

Perspiration: Use enzyme detergent or chlorine bleach solution.

Plasticine: Remove deposit, then use dry-cleaner or lighter fuel.

Rust: Use lemon juice and salt and dry in the sun.

Scorch marks: Sponge with borax/hydrogen peroxide or ammonia solution.

Tar: Remove deposit, then use eucalyptus oil.

Tea: See Coffee.

Unidentified stains: Have these professionally dry-cleaned.

Vomit: See dog or cat messes.

Wine: Cover with salt or flush red wine stain with white wine. Next day, use borax or enzyme detergent solution.

Yoghurt: Remove deposit, then use dry-cleaner.

Entertaining

Need an excuse..?

Dinner Party
Rock 'n' Roll Party
Pirates Party
Sixties Party
Hawaiian Party
Fondue Party
Valentine's Day Party
Guy Fawkes Party
Hallowe'en Party
New Year's Eve Party
First Pheasant Party
Hire a Film Party
Coffee Morning
Gambling Party
Garden Party
April Fools Party
Bon Voyage Party
Picnic
Heroes and Villains
   Party
Comic Strip Party

Roman Orgy
After Dinner Drink
Come As You Are
   Party
Blondes Have More
   Fun Party
Shakespearian Party
Name-drop Party
Cocktail Party
Current Affairs Party
Masked Ball
At Home
Patriotic Party
Fund-raising Party
St Trinians Party
Tea Party
Bad Taste Party
Futuristic Party
Barbecue
Wine and Cheese
   Party

Party facts and figures

It is better to hold your party in one crowded room than in two half empty rooms.

An empty room will hold roughly 1 person to every 0.5 square metres (5 square feet) of floor space.

In an empty hall, allow roughly 1 person to every 0.75 square metres (8 square feet) of floor space.

Around a table, allow about 60cm (24 inches) of table width per person. (Round tables are best for capacity and ease of conversation.)

Allow 16–20 glasses from a bottle of sherry.

Allow 18 drinks from a bottle of whisky.

Allow 20 drinks from a bottle of gin.

At a cocktail party, allow 8 canapés and 3–4 drinks per person, plus a few extra.

At a cocktail party allow half a bottle of wine per head, and some extra.

At an adult tea party, allow 3–4 savoury items, 2 small cakes or slices of cake and 2 cups of tea per person.

Arrange for dinner parties to start approximately half an hour after guests arrive.

Unless guests know each other well, a maximum age range of ten years is advisable.

Aim at having equal numbers of men and women.

Invite guests to a large party between 10 days and 3 weeks before the event.

Party countdown

3–4 weeks beforehand

How much money do you want to spend?

How many people are you planning to invite? (The more people you invite, the more it will cost – or the simpler your party will have to be.)

What will you give your guests to drink?

Do you want to buy or make the food?

Are you going to need help (hired or from friends)?

Will you need to book music or entertainment?

What sort of party do you want to give?

At what time of day will the party take place?

How long do you want your guests to stay?

Where will you hold the party?

Will the party have a specific theme?

Is it to celebrate anything in particular?

How and when are you going to invite your guests?

Do you need an RSVP?

Have you booked caterers, barmen, entertainment, rented a space and invited your guests?

1 week beforehand Have you made a list of what still has to be done?

Have you thought about music, food, drink, decorations, help and you (costume, outfit)?

Have you found out how many guests are coming? (If you need to invite more, do so now.)

Have you warned or invited your neighbours?

Have you worked out how much drink you'll need and ordered it? See *Party facts and figures* (page 196).

Have you asked guests to bring a bottle? (Remember, not everyone drinks alcohol, so you should supply soft drinks as well.)

Have you planned the atmosphere you want to create and worked out how to achieve it?

Have you hired or bought glasses, plates, cutlery, decorations and furniture, etc?

Have you got enough ashtrays and rubbish bags?

Have you borrowed or hired a sound system and/or lights?

Have you got enough record albums/tapes?

Have you got the correct plugs, cables and screwdrivers?

Have you checked that your arrangements with caterer, disco, barmen and others still hold?

1–2 days beforehand Complete food buying (including ice).

Prepare as much food as possible.

Borrow serving dishes and plates if necessary.

Remove excess furniture from the room(s) and position remaining pieces.

Arrange lighting (at the same time of day as the party).

Buy special light bulbs, candles, toilet paper, paper napkins.

Decide where guests will leave their coats and which bathroom they will use.

Select music.

Position sound system and note optimum sound level.

Remove and lock up anything valuable.

Spring clean.

Put out ashtrays.

Find the tablecloths you will need.

3 hours beforehand Fill fridge with drink that needs to be served cold.

Make any last-minute dishes.

Put out glasses, plates, cutlery, napkins, bottles (and corkscrew) and food.

Open red wine.

Position lamps for best effect and turn them on.

Locate spare bulbs or fuses.

Make sure room(s) are warm (or cool) enough.

Look critically around room(s) and see if you've missed anything.

Lie down with a drink and relax.

Shower and change.

Put on some restful music.

Admire the scene.

Sit down and accept that there's nothing else you can do now.

Sorry, can't make it

Upset stomach
Parents just 'phoned . . . they're coming that weekend
Can't find a babysitter
Car won't start
The dog's sick
Nothing to wear
Jury service
Working late
The boss invited us for dinner
Partner is feeling rather ill
Ring the day after to ask if it's next week
Got drunk at lunch
Lost my contact lenses
Have tickets for the theatre
Ring the day after – fell asleep

Ideal drinks cabinet

Whisky
Gin
Vodka
White rum
Dark rum
Pernod
Sweet vermouth
Dry vermouth
Cinzano
Campari
Sweet sherry
Dry sherry
Port
Cognac
Armagnac

Grand Marnier
Red wine
White wine
Dessert wine
Champagne
Case of lager (or
   other beer)
Soda water
Tonic water
Bitter lemon
Coke
Dry ginger
Orange juice
Tomato juice

Basic cocktail kit

Good recipe book
Drink measures
Mixer or shaker
Strainer
Blender
Lemon squeezer
Sharp knife
Ice tongs
Chopping board
White linen napkin
  (for style)
Cocktail glasses
Cocktail spoon
Swizzle sticks
Japanese parasols
Crushed ice
Lemons

Limes
Oranges
Maraschino cherries
Angostura bitters
Olives
Onions
Fresh mint
Cucumber
Grenadine
Cassis
Worcestershire
  sauce
Sugar syrup
Fruit juices
Sugar
Salt

Getting rid of a hangover

Try drinking lots of black coffee . . .
. . . or water
. . . or sweet tea
. . . or coke
. . . or champagne
. . . or a digestive
. . . or a Prairie Oyster (raw egg, dash of tabasco, dash of Worcestershire sauce, salt and pepper mixed together), drunk in one gulp
. . . or lemon and honey
. . . or go back to bed and sleep
Next time, drink lots of water before you go to bed.

Formal table laying

Place setting (right to left)

Small knife (for bread or hors d'œuvres)

Soup spoon

Fish knife

Large knife (for main course)

Dessert spoon

Plate (remains for entire meal, and other plates are placed on top)

Teaspoon (rests on plate, if required for first course such as grapefruit or prawn cocktail)

Dessert fork

Large fork (for main course)

Fish fork

Small fork (for hors d'œuvres)

Side plate

Napkin (above side plate, use linen or cotton rather than paper)

Small knife (placed on napkin if other small knife is for hors d'œuvres)

Finger bowl (placed on the left, above the line of forks)

Water tumbler (just above the blade of the large knife)

Red wine glass (next to tumbler)

White wine glass (next to red wine glass)

Port glass (or bring it in when the port is served)

Extras

Place cards (if the party is large or very formal)

Place mats/tablecloth (or both, if you have to protect your table, yet want to use a cloth)

Flowers (must be short-stemmed and not highly scented)

Candles (at a formal dinner use white candles, if any)

Ashtrays (if you don't object to your guests smoking during the meal)

Salt-cellars and pepper-pots (roughly one set for every four guests)

Mustard-pots (roughly one for every four guests)

Any other condiments

Butter dishes (and butter knives)

Serving spoons (as many as you need)

Serving forks

Remember to remove salt, pepper, mustard, etc from the table before serving dessert.

How to enjoy your dinner party

When guests arrive, serve a few generous drinks.

Invite one or two talkative friends.

Work out your table plan in advance.

Make sure you have enough plates and cutlery.

Remember the size of your oven and hob.

Don't have too many courses.

Prepare everything beforehand.

Never cook anything that could turn out a complete disaster.

Serve food direct from the oven in beautiful gratin dishes.

Have a cold first course.

Serve a casserole or roast as a main course.

Have a salad instead of vegetables.

Eat cheese and fruit, or an exotic ice cream, instead of an elaborate dessert.

Leave your sink filled with hot, soapy water and put the used plates in it to soak.

If possible, wash up as you go along.

Make sure you don't run out of food or drink; allow for two 'extra' guests, and never rely on guests to bring wine.

Wine rules

Serve white wine before red wine.
Serve a light wine before a heavy one.
Serve a young wine before an old one.
Serve dry wine before sweet wine.
Serve an expensive wine before a cheaper one.

Weekend guests

Have you told them whether it's snowing or sunny, so that they can pack accordingly?

Have you cleared away the junk in the guest room?

Have you aired and made their beds?

Have you seen if there's any space in the wardrobe and found a few spare coat hangers?

Have you dug out clean towels and bought a spare toothbrush, in case they forget theirs?

Have you made sure the lights work in their bedroom?

Have you turned on the radiators and found electric blankets or hot water bottles?

Have you put magazines and a bunch of flowers on the bedside table?

Have you left a jug of water and some chocolates or biscuits in their room?

Have you done all the shopping, so they don't feel they have to contribute?

Have you prepared as much food as possible, so you won't spend the entire weekend in the kitchen?

Have you arranged some nice things for them to do?

Have you found all your old maps and guide books of the area?

Children's party shopping

Invitations
Balloons (lots)
Streamers
Candles and candle holders
Crackers
Paper party hats
Whistles and blowers
Small gifts and prizes (books, mugs, soaps, pencils)
Wrapping paper, sellotape, labels (for pass-the-parcel and presents)
Music of some sort (for musical bumps and sing-alongs)
Paper tissues and kitchen towels
Coloured drinking straws
Paper plates, mugs and napkins
Plastic cutlery
Crêpe paper tablecloth
Big waste paper bags (for collecting rubbish)
Small tables and chairs (if necessary, hire them)
Birthday cake
Cake decoration
Sweets
Drink
Food

Hints for children's parties

Try not to invite more children than the age of the birthday child!

Let your child provide a guest list.

Don't forget to invite those children who have invited your child to parties in the past.

Make sure all guests are approximately the same age.

Invite similar-aged relatives.

Decide on a time for the party to end and stick to it. (Children's parties normally last from 3–6 pm. Parties for young children should end sooner.)

Mention on the invitation that you will take children home. (This way, the party can end promptly and you won't need to entertain other parents.)

Arrange drinks and food for any parent who has to collect a child.

Ask at least one other adult to help you.

Allow one adult for every ten children.

Forget about cleaning before the party, clean afterwards.

Make space – remove furniture or push it against the walls.

Roll up the carpet or cover it with an old sheet (especially under the dining table).

Use two rooms, one for games and one for eating in.

Remove all breakable objects from both rooms.

Watch out for trailing lamp cords, unguarded electrical sockets, etc. See *Keep your children safe* (page 160).

Lock all cupboards and remove the keys.

Decorate the place with lots of balloons, streamers, etc.

Use disposable paper plates, mugs, napkins, tablecloth and cutlery.

Buy ready-made cakes and instant desserts, and save your creativity for decorating them.

Make a stunning-looking birthday cake. (Be sure your ballet theme isn't last year's fad and they are really into cricket now.)

Buy lots of matches to light and relight birthday cake candles.

Make sure that you've got enough sweets, balloons, crayons, etc so that each guest can win lots of fun prizes and also have a present to take home.

Keep stain removing book, mop and good clothes brush handy.

Work out the programme of games before children arrive – don't leave one second unplanned!

When children arrive, keep each child's coat, hat, scarf and shoes together to make sure that they can be found when it's time to leave.

Play active games before tea and quieter ones after.

If you are hiring a professional entertainer, arrange to have the performance directly after tea.

Make sure that the last event is a quiet one so that they can calm down before going home.

Do have a first aid box and a spare bed prepared, just in case one of the guests gets too excited.

Children's party catering

Under 5 years old
Marmite, egg and jam sandwiches (with the crusts cut off)
Chocolate biscuits
Jelly or blancmange
Ice cream
Plain sponge birthday cake with icing and candles
Butterfly and fairy cakes
Milk
Orangeade

5 to 8 years old
Bridge rolls with egg and meat paste fillings
Biscuits with savoury spreads
Sausages on sticks
Grapes or pineapple and cheese on sticks
Crisps or funny-shaped potato crackers
Ice cream
Trifle

Sponge cakes (put their names on top with icing)
Fruit juices
Coke
Milk
Birthday cake (make it in an interesting shape)

9 to 12 years old
Fish and chips
Hamburgers
Pizzas

Hot dogs
Sausages on sticks
Grapes or pineapple and cheese on sticks
Ice cream
Coke
Fruit juices
Birthday cake with candles (only use a theme if you think your child would like it)

For children over 9 years old, food should look as adult as possible.

Ten party games

Musical bumps: All the children jump up and down to music. When it stops, they sit on the floor, and the last child down is out. The winner is the last one left.

Fishes: The children are divided into two teams. Two fish are cut out of paper and one is given to each team. The teams are also given a folded newspaper. The idea is to flap the newspaper so that the fish move across the room and back again. The team whose fish finishes first is the winner.

Musical chairs: The same number of chairs as the number of children are put in a long row, and one is removed. The children dance round the chairs to music and when music stops they have to sit on a chair. The child left standing is out, and another chair is removed. The winner is the child who sits on the last chair.

Balloon game: Two teams are formed and the object of the game is to pass a blown balloon from child to child down the line, using knees only and without bursting the balloon. The fastest team wins.

Sardines: One child hides and the others try to find him. Once they succeed, they hide with him. The last child to find the others, hides next.

Pass the parcel: Beforehand, wrap a present in several layers of paper and secure each layer with sellotape. At the party, while music is playing, the parcel is passed round a circle of children. When the music stops, the child holding the parcel starts quickly to unwrap it. Ten seconds later the music starts again and the parcel is passed around until the music stops. The child who finally unwraps the present, keeps it.

Beetles: Two teams are given a dice, paper, pencil and an adult to supervise. The idea is to throw the dice and be the first team to draw the beetle: a 6 builds the body; 5, the head; 4, one of the six legs; 3, one of the two antlers; 2, the tail; 1, one of two eyes.

Musical statues: This is similar to Musical Bumps, only less energetic. The last person to stand still when the music stops is out, and so on until only one child is left.

Egg and spoon race: As its name suggests, each player has a spoon and a hard-boiled egg. On the signal, without using hands, each player must pick up the egg in the spoon and run to the finishing line. This game is best played out of doors.

Dead soldiers: All the children, except two, lie on the floor pretending to be dead. The other two must try and make them laugh or move, without touching them. The winner is the last child to remain still.

Don't forget to buy prizes, and make sure all the children get one.

Holidays

Choosing a holiday

Sightseeing: Worthwhile, but hard on the feet!

Romantic: Better with two, if it works out the way you planned!

Exotic: Exciting, take camera and insect repellent!

Exploring: Adventurous, but consider why has no-one been there before?

Driving: Freedom, if you can stand the pace!

A cruise: Luxurious, but do you get sea-sick?

Sporty: Great for the figure, but wouldn't you rather relax?

Group holiday: New friends . . . or enemies?

With friends: Well done, if you're still friends by the end!

Alone: Good way to meet people, but potentially dangerous.

Self-catering: Cheap and flexible, so long as you don't have to cook!

Stay at home: Sunshine not guaranteed, but you know the menu!

Beach: Fine, if you like sand in your shoes and making your neighbours jealous!

Camping: Back to basics, fresh air, and ants in the butter!

Bicycling: Great way to see the country, if the rain doesn't get in your eyes!

Carnival-time: Fun time to be there, but be prepared to be ripped off.

Gourmet: Delicious, but don't forget to book a visit to a health farm as well!

Language-learning: Hard work, but at least you will eventually be able to understand the train time-table.

Mountaineering: Spectacular views for those with sturdy legs and a head for heights.

Canal: Great fun, if your crew doesn't mutiny.

How much will it cost?

Holiday costs

Basic charge per person (as quoted in brochure)	£
Surcharge conditions (fuel, increase in airport charges, etc)	£
Currency surcharge (if £ falls dramatically)	£
Supplements on room cost (TV, single room, sea view, bathroom, etc)	£
Airport charges (taxes, excess baggage, etc)	£
Extras (lunch, rented car, etc)	£
Total cost	£

Reductions

Group reduction, if relevant	£
Children's reductions, if relevant	£
Saving gained by changing dates (travelling mid-week or the week before)	£
Any special reductions	£
Total reduction	£
Grand total (subtract total reduction from total cost)	£

How to save money

Compare costs.

Book in advance (or at the last minute) and try for a discount.

Holiday off-season, but check the weather first.

Travel to a 'cheap' country, everything will cost less.

Go to any country with a currency weaker than ours, or to a country that has just devalued its currency.

Take a package holiday.

Travel with friends or family rather than alone – it tends to be cheaper this way.

Go on a group holiday.

Travel by bus, coach, train or bike.

If flying, take a charter flight.

Don't have excess baggage.

Reserve the cheapest hotel room.

Don't have room service, tempting as it may be.

Stick to the check-out time or you may have to pay for another day.

Always book hotels in advance, never take pot-luck. You could end up sleeping in the Hilton or on the beach!

If travelling by car, make sure the hotel gives you free parking.

Avoid taxis.

Stay in youth hostels or with friends.
Remember to invite them to stay with you too.

Rent a villa or chalet rather than staying in an hotel.

Take as much as you can with you, such as toothpaste, plasters, etc, so you don't have to buy things there.

Eat fixed price meals rather than à la carte.

Holiday tips

Don't give your phone number to all the delicious men/women you meet. (You might not appreciate their turning up on your doorstep a few weeks later.)

Don't lie on the beach all day when you first arrive. (Lobsters are not very attractive.)

Don't read too engrossing a book at the airport. (You might miss the plane.)

Don't scream at foreigners in English if they don't understand you. (Scream at them in their own language.)

Don't eat everything they do. (Your stomach probably isn't up to it.)

Don't leave home without knowing anything about where you're going. (It might come as rather a shock.)

Don't get upset if everything isn't the same as it is in England. (That's what you went away for.)

Don't hitch-hike unless you really have to. (You wouldn't do it at home.)

Don't gesticulate wildly when abroad. (It might mean something completely different over there.)

Don't quench your thirst with the tap water in your hotel room. (You never know where it has come from.)

International time (Winter)

City	Time	City	Time
Adelaide	+9	Brussels	+1
Berlin	+1	Calcutta	$+5\frac{1}{2}$
Bern	+1	Chicago	−6
Bombay	$+5\frac{1}{2}$	Dublin	GMT
Boston	−5	Florence	+1

City	Time	City	Time
Istanbul	+1	Perth	+8
Jerusalem	+2	Philadelphia	−5
Leningrad	+3	Prague	+1
Lisbon	GMT	Quebec	−5
London	GMT	Rome	+1
Madras	+5½	Rotterdam	+1
Madrid	+1	San Francisco	−8
Malta	+1	Sydney	+10
Melbourne	+10	Stockholm	+1
Moscow	+3	Tokyo	+9
New York	−5	Toronto	−5
Paris	+1	Vancouver	−8
Peking	+8	Vienna	+1

Time is shown in hours fast (+) or slow (−) of GMT (Greenwich Mean Time).

Before you go...

Book your holiday and collect the tickets.

Check your passport is still valid, and get a new one if it isn't.

Make sure you've got the relevant visas.

Check if you need any vaccinations, injections or malaria preventatives.

Order travellers' cheques and/or foreign currency.

Get an International Driving Licence, if necessary.

Service your car, if taking it, and check insurance documentation, etc.

Check whether you are sufficiently insured against theft, medical costs, etc, and if not take out extra insurance.

Book your pets in with friends, or into a kennel.

Arrange for someone to stay in your home while you are away.

Pay all your bills early so you don't get 'disconnected' while you are away.

Read *Don't leave without* . . . (opposite), and buy what you need.

Find out what the weather is like where you're going and pack accordingly.

Make a list of the serial numbers of your possessions in case your house is burgled when you are away. See *Serial numbers to keep* (page 120).

Write an itinerary and leave it with your friends, relatives and work place.

Ask the post office to hold your mail.

Tell your neighbours and the police when and for how long you will be away.

Leave your house key with neighbours.

Arrange to have your lawn mowed if you're going away for a long time.

Ask your neighbours to water your plants, or splash out and buy some self-watering plant pots.

Buy an automatic light switch and attach it to your radio and a light.

Cancel the papers and milk.

Lock up your ladders.

De-frost and clean out your fridge if it's going to be a long holiday.

Unplug all electrical appliances (except the automatic light switch).

Turn off the gas supply.

Shut and bolt all windows and doors.

Medication to take abroad

Travel sickness pills
Sun tan lotion, with heavy screen for fair skins
Antiseptic cream
Crêpe bandage
Gauze bandage
Cotton wool
Assorted plasters
Soluble aspirin or paracetamol
Insect repellent
Mild steroid cream (for bites)
Antacid (for stomach aches and heartburn)
Calamine lotion
Mild laxative
Anti-diarrhoeal tablets (for turista/ Montezuma's revenge)
Salt tablets (if you are going somewhere very hot)
Water-purifying tablets
Any drugs you take regularly

It is a good idea to carry with you a copy of any prescription you are likely to need. Make sure the generic name of the drug is on the prescription as brand names vary.

Once again, do check that you have adequate medical insurance.

Don't leave without...

Your tickets (there and back)
Passport(s) with relevant visa(s)
Vaccination certificates, if relevant
Foreign currency
Travellers' cheques
Credit cards
English money (for when you return)
Safety belt (for valuables)
Travel Insurance Policy
International Driving Licence, if necessary
Address book (Make sure it includes your bank's address and the addresses of any friends you have in the area you intend to visit.)
Travel guide and list of recommended restaurants and sights
Luggage contents check list (to check that you've packed

everything when you leave, or to help you make a claim if your suitcase gets lost)

Miniature first aid kit. (See *Medication to take abroad*, page 217.)

Clothes sizes of family and friends (for presents)

Nylon bag (for souvenirs)

Needle, thread and safety pins

Travel iron

Pencil, paper, games and two packs of playing cards

Camera and film

Books

Miniature alarm clock and a radio

Adaptable electric socket, if necessary

Hot water bottle, if you feel the cold

Water bottle

Penknife (the one that opens cans, cuts your fingernails, etc)

Take sunglasses, raincoat, walking shoes, skis, etc, depending where you are going.

Make a list of all important numbers: passport, bank account, travellers' cheques, credit cards, etc and keep it on you in case your things get stolen.

Packing hints

Make a list of all the clothes, jewellery, etc that you are taking with you.

Stuff your shoes with socks/tights/knickers to save space and to keep your shoes from collapsing.

Place shoes (in shoe bags) and other heavy items at the bottom of your case on the side opposite the handle, so that they are at the bottom when the case is upright.

Fold jumpers, T-shirts, lingerie and towels lengthwise, individually, and then roll them up to stop them creasing.

Roll jewellery, cameras and other fragile articles inside the rolled clothes for protection.

Keep leather belts flat and put them along the sides of your case; they may crack if folded.

Pack toiletries at the bottom of your case surrounded with padding so that they cannot break. Don't take heavy bottles, decant them. Make sure all toiletries are in a special case or plastic bag in case they break.

Pack trousers by placing the waist band to the side of the case leaving the legs hanging outside. Place the next pair in the opposite direction and then fold the legs of the first pair into the case over the second pair of trousers, and then the legs of the second pair on top of those of the first. This method prevents creasing. Do the same with skirts.

Put socks in the collars of men's shirts to keep collars from creasing.

Place folded shirts in the case so that the collar is on a different side of the case each time.

Pack dresses lengthwise, folded at the waist, with the skirt on the bottom.

Lie jackets face up in the case, with the collar to the middle of the case and the buttons done up. Fold the sleeves on top of the jacket, keeping them as straight as possible and pointing towards the bottom of the jacket. Then fold up the bottom of the jacket.

Pack delicate items of clothing (eg silk shirts) on top.

Always lock your case and keep the key in a safe place.

Always keep the list of the contents of your case with you. Your case may get lost and you might need to make a claim.

Travelling games

Anything to do with spotting car number plates.

Guessing how many legs there will be on the next pub sign.

Telling all the jokes you know.

Animal, Vegetable or Mineral.

Start by telling a story, stop at an exciting bit and let the next person continue the story, and so on.

I Spy.

Guessing how many cars you will pass in the next mile going in the opposite direction, and then counting them.

Alphabet game: list animals, cities, rivers, countries, etc that start with the same letter.

Guessing how far away an object is in the distance by predicting what the mileage will be when you reach it.

Memory game: start with a word/phrase (When I went to China, I took with me a . . .). The next person has to repeat what you've said and add a word, and so on.

Noughts and crosses.

Reverse noughts and crosses (being the last to get three in a row).

Hangman.

Battleships.

Patience.

Always take a packet of sweets as a bribe (or prize).

Take some cassettes with you to sing along to.

weddings

Your wedding

First, decide who is going to do the decision-making – you or the bride's parents. Or will you divide the responsibility?

How much do you want to spend? (Who's paying?)

Do you want a small or a large ceremony?

Do you want a small wedding and reception one day and followed by a larger party another day.

Do you want only family and close friends to attend, or other people as well?

Do you want a double wedding?

Do you want it to be formal or informal?

What time of year do you want to be married? (Consider tax implications as well as more romantic ones.)

How many months will you need for planning? (Three months is considered the best length of time.)

Where do you want to get married?

Where would you like to hold your reception?

What do you want to do at the reception?

Do you want music? If so what kind?

What day of the week would you prefer to get married on?

What time of day would you prefer for the wedding?

Do you want a colour theme to your wedding?

Bride's family expenditure

Press announcements	£
Bride's wedding dress, veil and accessories	£
Bride's attendants' wedding clothes	£
Flowers for the church and reception	£
Engagement and wedding photographs	£
Transportation of bridal party to church and reception	£
Groom's wedding ring	£
Groom's wedding present	£
The reception, including food, drink, music, decorations, professional services, etc	£
Room in which the bride can change into going-away outfit	£
Wedding cake	£
After the reception, the posting of slices of wedding cake to friends who did not attend	£
Printing and postage of all invitations, announcements, etc	£
Printing of the Order of Service	£
Total	£

Bridesmaids may wish to pay for their own clothes, especially if they will be wearing something they can wear again.

Consider sharing the cost of the church flowers with any other couples marrying in the same church on the same day as you.

Bridegroom's expenditure

All fees connected with the church, except floral decorations	£
The buying or hiring of groom's wedding outfit	£
Bride's bouquet and going-away flowers	£
Bouquets for the attendants	£
Flower sprays for mothers, and perhaps also grandmothers	£
Button holes for himself and the other male members of the wedding party	£
Bride's engagement and wedding rings	£
Bride's wedding present	£
Gifts for attendants and best man	£
Honeymoon	£
Total	£

If you're not plagued by tradition, it is a good idea to consider splitting the costs of the wedding more evenly between the two families, or paying for it all yourselves. Whatever you do, don't hurt the feelings of the bride's parents.

If you are considering splitting costs, split the cost of the honeymoon too, as you probably will split the cost of most of your shared holidays in the future.

The professionals

The minister, priest, rabbi or registrar
Church organist, bell-ringers and choir
Printer or stationer
Florist
Photographer
Dressmaker (for bride's wedding dress)
Clothes hire company (for men's clothes)
Jeweller (for the rings)
Car-hire company
Local hotel manager or caterer
Marquee hire company
Musicians (for the reception)
Wedding gift consultant (at local department store)

Bride's wedding countdown

3 months   Make all the decisions you can at this early stage. Read *Your wedding* (page 222).

Choose a date and time for the wedding.

With your fiancé, see the minister, priest, rabbi or registrar to arrange the wedding.

Think about what hymns and other music you want before, during and after the ceremony.

Shop around for an hotel or caterers, and book them.

If you want music at the reception, book the musicians.

With your fiancé and both sets of parents, make a guest list.

Arrange transport for the day, either with a local car-hire firm or with friends.

Book a photographer whose work you like.

Order your wedding cake, unless the hotel or caterer is doing this for you.

Order the printed or engraved invitations. Start addressing the envelopes the moment you receive them.

With your fiancé, choose bridesmaids, ushers and the best man.

Choose your wedding dress and all the other wedding clothes.

Pick and order dresses for your attendants.

Discuss honeymoon plans with your fiancé and start making reservations.

2 months   Confirm food and drink arrangements with hotel or caterer.

Find a florist and order flowers to match your wedding colour scheme. Make sure they are in season.

Let your mother and future mother-in-law know the predominant colour so that they can choose their dresses now.

Go shopping with your fiancé for your wedding ring.

Consult your minister about your choice of wedding music and make an appointment to see the organist.

Order your printed service sheets and arrange for them to be delivered to your best man about a week before the wedding.

4–6 weeks before the wedding send out the invitations. Include the bridegroom's family and the vicar and his wife.

Make a list of the wedding presents you would like. Either send a copy to all your friends (this method needs organising to ensure they don't all choose the same present) or leave the list at several shops or stores of your choice.

Buy personal stationery for thank-you letters and write immediately you receive a gift.

If sending souvenir wedding cake, order special boxes from a stationer.

Go shopping for your going-away and honeymoon clothes.

If you wish to change the name in your passport, allow six weeks.

List the acceptances and refusals.

1 month Confirm the final number of guests with the hotel or caterer, in writing.

Check that the car-hire company, photographer and florist are ordered and correctly briefed.

Arrange sleeping accommodation and transport for friends who live far away.

With your fiancé, choose gifts for the attendants.

Have a full dress rehearsal, where the wedding will take place, if possible.

Work out how long it will take for you to get to the church on the day, and allow for delays.

Buy a wedding present for your fiancé.

Arrange to have your honeymoon case sent to the place where the reception is to be held if you are leaving for your holiday from there.

Double-check that the wedding dress fits.

Try out your hairstyle and book an appointment with your hairdresser for the morning of your wedding.

If you want to, send your wedding announcement to the papers.

Best man's role

He must check arrangements with the bride's family from time to time.

He should arrange the stag night if the groom wants one, but preferably not the night before the wedding, and ensure that the groom gets home safely.

He has to check that the ushers know their responsibilities.

He must see that the buttonholes and service sheets are at the church, ready to be handed out to guests when they arrive.

He should arrange that the groom's going-away and honeymoon clothes are packed and taken to the hotel or reception hall on the morning of the wedding.

He must drive the bridegroom to church, and pay the church fees, etc on behalf of the groom on arrival at the church.

He must check that he has the ring, and hand it to the minister or groom at the appropriate moment.

He must, with the ushers, organise transport and/or parking for all the guests.

He must liaise with the toastmaster on the order of speeches and decide on a good time to announce the cutting of the cake.

He may make a speech, but in any case he should read telegrams and congratulations, and thank the groom for his toast to the bridesmaids.

Questions and answers

1. May my fiancé(e), who is divorced, and I marry in church?
You may in certain non-conformist churches, but not in the Church of England nor in the Roman Catholic Church.

2. When should I lift my veil back from over my face?
In the vestry when you go to sign the register.

3. Where can I hire a wedding dress?
Consult the Yellow Pages or *Brides* magazine.

4. Which comes first, the speeches or the cutting of the cake?
The cake is cut before the speeches so that it may be sliced in time to hand around after the toasts.

5. Can I wear white for a second marriage?
Yes, if you want to.

6. Who sits where at the top table?
From right to left: Best man/Groom's mother/

Bride's father/Bride/Groom/Bride's mother/
Groom's father/Bridesmaid.

7. Must my husband wear a morning suit if I wear a long white dress?
No, he can wear a dark, formal lounge suit.

8. Must I have been christened to be married in church?
One or other of you must have been christened to enable you to marry in church.

9. How do I store my wedding dress?
Fold it flat in layers of black tissue paper, wrap it in black cloth or more tissue paper and store the box, flat, in a place that is dark, dry and cool.

10. What do I do with my engagement ring during the ceremony?
Keep it on the third finger of your right hand.

List of ten most frequently asked questions kindly compiled by Brides *magazine.*

Wedding anniversaries

1 year: paper	12 years: linen
2 years: cotton	13 years: lace
3 years: leather	14 years: ivory
4 years: flowers	15 years: crystal
5 years: wood	20 years: china
6 years: iron	25 years: silver
7 years: wool	30 years: pearl
8 years: bronze	40 years: ruby
9 years: pottery	50 years: gold
10 years: aluminium	60 years: diamond
11 years: steel	

Money

How to save money

See your situation as a challenge rather than an embarrassment.

Make a game of seeing who in the family can economise most.

Try and cut down on large sums, rather than on small fun luxuries.

Look after your possessions and make sure they last longer.

Be sensible – don't drive 20 miles to buy cheaper vegetables.

Don't always buy cheaper items – they are not necessarily good buys.

Never impulse buy – always shop around and do as much market research as you can before buying.

Experiment with food – use produce in season, eat in, not out, and take sandwiches to work and school.

Try and cut down on gas and electricity consumption.

Use your telephone only when cheap rates apply – and keep calls short.

Buy a bicycle and sell your car (your body will benefit too).

Have holidays at home instead of abroad.

Stop spending when your purse is empty – avoid using cheque-books or credit cards.

Keep enough money in the bank to avoid paying bank charges.

Be good to bank managers

Keep your account in the black.

Show him that you are capable of handling your finances.

Don't overspend – and try not to draw cheques when funds are not available to meet them.

Make an arrangement to be overdrawn – before it happens.

Apologise if you are in the red.

Always make an appointment to see him – and be punctual.

Let him know in advance what you want to discuss.

Do your homework beforehand and take him as many facts and figures as possible.

If you want to borrow money, make sure you know how much you need to borrow, tell him what it is for and how you are going to repay it.

If you want to borrow money, demonstrate that you can provide security for the loan.

Do not expect your enthusiasm to influence your bank manager – he will want something more concrete.

To make a good impression, work out your budget before going to see him. See *Work out your budget* (page 238).

If, after following the above advice, you are still intimidated by, or on bad terms with, your bank manager, change banks. Nice bank managers do exist!

Thinking about a lodger?

Do you need money, like company or both?

Does your lease permit you to take a lodger?

Do you mind taking a risk if it doesn't?

Do you want a male or female lodger?

What have you got to offer space-wise?

Do you mind losing your privacy?

Which rooms, if any, will you share with them and with what limitations?

Think about your idiosyncracies and make sure you will be able to keep them.

Do you mind a smoker if you are a non-smoker, or a meat-eater if you are vegetarian?

Will you offer any meals?

Will you supply clean linen and towels?

Will the lodger have space to do washing or is there a launderette nearby?

Will you clean the lodger's room?

Do you mind the lodger using your telephone?

Do you want a short- or long-term lodger?

How will you find your lodger? (Through friends, local hospital, technical college, etc.)

How much rent will you charge?

Do you want weekly or monthly rent payments?

Remember to keep rent-paying orderly.

Remember to ask for the rent for the first and last months in advance, or ask for a deposit.

Remember to ask for references if the prospective lodger is not a friend.

Your accountant needs...

General   Synopsis of your financial and personal history over the last ten years or so, if you are a new client.

For tax return preparation

Any tax certificates you have:

Income from employment (salary), P60 or P45

Income from building societies

Income from shares (dividend vouchers)

Income from trusts, etc

A list of all sources of income:

Salary (including partner's)

Details of company car (Form P11D from employer), include details of reimbursements received from employer and amount still out of pocket

Self-employed income (see *If self-employed*, page 235) or freelance income

Bank deposit account(s)

Building society account(s)

Details of shares owned (number of shares, date of purchase and cost price)

Trust income

Details of pensions

Income from property

Details of any assets sold (date of sale, cost price and date of purchase, proceeds)

A list of all outgoings:

Mortgage/loan interest on home

Any other interest paid

Life Insurance paid

Pension contributions

Alimony/maintenance

Deeds of Covenant

Children/dependants supported

Details of tax district/reference number.

Any communications from the Inland Revenue.

Preparing information thoroughly and presenting it in an orderly state will help your accountant and reduce your bill!

Remember your accountant is on your side; don't be afraid to give him all the information.

Don't forget to ask your accountant questions too. Make sure he helps you plan ways to ease the preparation of detailed information and to reduce tax!

Ask him whether you should be making any changes to your existing tax affected income/ outgoings.

Ask him about whatever is worrying you.

Remember that the tax year runs from 6 April to the following 5 April, so start working on your accounts after Christmas or, better still, do it monthly!

If self-employed

General   Read and prepare everything relevant from *Your accountant needs . . .* (above).

For tax return preparation   Have your books up to date, if you can do this.

Give accountant all your invoices and receipts, clearly labelled to show what they were for, and supporting bank statements.

Prepare an analysis of expenses:

(a) Your car

Year and make of car

Date you purchased car

Total amount of miles driven

Amount of business miles driven

Amount of personal miles driven

Cost of petrol and oil this year

Cost of insurance

Cost of repairs and servicing

Cost of road tax and resident's parking permit

Cost of parking (meters, fines, etc)

HP payments cost

Cost of car club memberships (AA/RAC, etc)

(b) Items specifically related to your business

Materials

Books

Postage/stationery

Travel costs

Magazines

Promotion/entertaining

Telephone

Insurances

Rent paid

Advertising

Sub-contract labour

Details of any equipment bought/hired

Professional fees (including legal and accountancy)

Any other other expenses (check with your accountant)

(c) Details of business trips

Destination

Purpose

Date of departure and arrival (UK)

Expenses on trip (fares, entertaining, etc)

(d) Your home

Rent/mortgate paid

General/water rates

Light/heat expenses

Decorating expenses and repairs

Cleaning expenses

Furniture used in business

Details of purchase or sale in year

Monthly finances

Check your bank statement(s). If there are errors, investigate.

Check that the bank has paid all your standing orders, the right amount, and at the right time.

Check that you know exactly how much money you have in your account(s).

Pay your overdue bills.

Check your building society book.

Check the progress of any money you have invested.

File all loose papers, correspondence, etc. See *Your filing system* (page 247).

If self-employed or working out your budget, collect receipts for the month and put them in an envelope.

Do your bookkeeping, if self-employed or for your own interest. Enter all the month's incomings and outgoings. Remember to enter any bank charges, investment income, etc.

If self-employed, send out any invoices for the month that you have not already dispatched.

Work out your budget

1. Find pencil, paper, rubber, pocket calcuator and spare batteries.

2. Grab partner and anyone else with whom you share finances – include children if you want to.

3. Work out what you would like to spend more money on if you had it, and where you would feel most happy economising, should you have to do so.

4. The first thing to do is to find out how much money you have coming in during the year.

5. Turn to *Annual income* (page 240), and fill it in as accurately as you can for every member of your family.

If unsure of a figure, always use a lower rather than a higher one – be realistic.

Never include a raise/bonus, etc until you've got it.

6. When the list is filled in, add up the figures to find your combined total yearly income. Then divide it by 12 to determine what you can spend monthly.

If you are unsure about next year's income (for example, if you are self-employed), include amounts you can predict accurately and, using them, work out a monthly average.

7. Turn to *Fixed expenses* (page 241), and fill in the list. As these are amounts you have to pay out, it is important to know exactly how much they are.

Work out each figure as a monthly expense (i.e. divide the half-yearly rates by 6, and the annual house insurance premium by 12).

8. When you've worked out the total of your monthly fixed expenses, subtract that amount from your monthly income.

9. The money left over should cover all your other expenses.

10. Turn to *Variable expenses* (page 242), and *Luxury expenses* (page 244), and read them.

11. You probably won't be able to fill them in accurately now, so for the next two weeks the whole family should keep a detailed record of how every penny is spent.

12. (Two weeks later) get out your pencil, rubber, paper, etc.

13. Collect everyone's detailed lists of how the money was spent, including cheque and credit card expenditure).

14. Fill in the *Variable expenses* list. Items on this list are important and probably cannot be avoided but they can be cut down. Bear in mind that with items such as the telephone, you will always have to pay rental and other fixed standing charges.

The 'Savings' entry needs to be carefully considered. Try to visualise your savings as an expense and budget accordingly. This will make it easier for you to save.

Try and maintain savings of two months of your annual income to be used only in times of emergency.

15. Work out your total *Variable expenses* expenditure per month and subtract it from the amount of money you had left over in item 9 above.

16. Now fill in the *Luxury expenses* list (page 244).

The 'Pocket Money' entry is only a suggestion. Decide how much each person should have monthly to spend on exactly what they want – a bit of privacy isn't a bad idea.

17. Once again, work out how much you spend per month and subtract it from the amount you had left.

18. You have now worked out your budget or simple cash flow analysis and can draw some conclusions.

Conclusions
If you have no money left, or were short, you may have muddled your arithmetic or you may be in a fairly critical financial position. Either way, consider taking drastic action.

If you have money left over, but not as much as you hoped, it is time you started living more frugally. See *How to save money* (page 231).

Consider which things you can most easily do without, or at least cut down on. Remember if you cross out an item 'on paper', you will have to do without it in real life too.

If you worked out that there should be money left over, but you know there isn't, try and find out what it has been spent on.

If you have adequate funds left over, try to plan an effective use for them. Your accountant or bank manager might be able to help you.

You now know how much money you can save and you can work out exactly what to cut down on in order to save more.

Always remember that these figures are not meant to dictate to you, but to help you. A budget should enable you to plan your money, not determine how you spend it.

Continue working out your budget whenever you feel like it (approximately every six months), but never let it become a chore.

Annual income

	per annum
Take home pay (after tax)	£
Any bonuses you regularly receive from work	£
Freelance work or overtime (if regular)	£
Child benefit	£
Maintenance (from ex-spouse or other source)	£
Rental income (lodger or grown-up children)	£

Dividends or interest from building society, shares, bank deposit account, etc	£
Regular cash gifts from relatives (only if you can depend on them)	£
Pension (private or service); grant	£
Any benefits you receive	£
Tax refunds due to you	£
Rate rebate	£
Rent rebate or allowance	£
Any profit you might make from the sale of your house, car, shares, etc (only if it is profit)	£
Any other income not included here	£
Total annual income	£
Divide by 12 for total monthly income	£

Fixed expenses

	per month
Mortgage payments	£
Ground rent or chief rent	£
Rates	£
Water rates	£
Repairs/redecoration/service charge	£
House insurance	£

Contents insurance	£
Endowment or Life Assurance	£
Hire purchase payments for furniture	£
National Insurance stamps, if self-employed	£
Fares to and from work	£
Union subscription or fee to professional body	£
Special clothing and tools for work, if necessary	£
Paternity payments	£
Maintenance payments to ex-spouse	£
Tax bills pending	£
Total monthly fixed expenses	£

Variable expenses

		per month
Heat/light	Electricity	£
	Gas	£
	Solid fuel	£
Food/drink	Bread (and other bakery products)	£
	Dairy produce	£
	Meat and fish	£
	Groceries	£

	Take-away food and off-licence drink	£
	Lunches at work	£
	School meals	£
Clothes	Men (include shoes and accessories)	£
	Women (include shoes and accessories)	£
	Children (include school uniform)	£
Cleaning	Laundry	£
	Dry-cleaning	£
	Cleaning materials	£
	Shoe repairs	£
	Domestic help/window cleaner, etc	£
Furnishings bought for cash	Curtains/rugs/upholstery, etc	£
	Kitchen gadgets, etc	£
	China/glass/silver, etc	£
	Wallpaper/paints, etc for home improvement	£
Communications	Telephone	£
	Postage	£
	Stationery	£
Professionals	Doctor and dentist	£
	Chemist	£
	Lawyer and accountant	£

Education	Children's school fees	£
	Fares to and from school	£
	Contributions to student grant	£
Others	Bank charges	£
	Savings (amount you want to save)	£
	Insurance (medical, etc)	£
	Total monthly variable expenses	£

Luxury expenses

	per month
Car expenses (See *The cost of car ownership,* page 125.)	£
Club memberships	£
Gardening expenses	£
Newspapers	£
Magazine subscriptions	£
Pet food/licence/vet's bills, etc	£
Toys	£
Television and video expenses	£
Sports equipment and lessons	£
Pocket money (for you and the children)	£

Gambling (pools, bingo, etc)	£
Cosmetics and hairdresser	£
Tobacco and chocolates	£
Luxury food and drink (including pubs and restaurants)	£
Holidays (annual and week-ends)	£
Entertaining	£
Cinema/theatre/concerts	£
Books/records/gifts	£
Music equipment and lessons	£
Any hobby expenditure	£
Total monthly luxury expenses	£

You

Your filing system

Keep locked up

Personal (certificates: birth, marriage, etc; love letters!).

Legal (anything involving your solicitor: your will, lease, etc).

Health (National Health cards, hospital cards, medical test results, list and dates of illnesses you have had, and any diets, health farms, etc on which you have decided to keep information).

Investments (details of shares, bonds, building society, etc).

Bank (statements, new and used cheque- and paying-in books, correspondence and Post Office savings book).

Credit cards (statements and correspondence).

Keep locked or unlocked

Home (all home-finances: bills for rates, mortgage, service charges, water, etc).

Post Office (telephone bills, TV and dog licences, etc).

Gas/Electricity (all bills and correspondence).

Insurance (property, contents, medical, etc.) Photograph your valuables and keep pictures here with a list of serial numbers (see *Serial numbers to keep,* page 120, and home contents (see *Insuring your home,* page 123).

Car (anything relevant: licence, service bills, MOT certificates, etc).

Guarantees (for all household appliances) and operating instructions, receipts, service addresses, etc.

Finance (anything concerning tax: coding notices, tax payments; incoming payments, etc).

Freelance work (copies of all invoices you've sent out and any work-related receipts).

Stores (statements and correspondence with any stores where you have an account).

Travel (foreign addresses, left-over currency, vaccination certificates and passport; also holiday price studies, and addresses of good travel agents).

Decoration (inspirational interiors pulled from magazines, paint and paper swatches, note of paints used, bills for furniture, carpets, etc to help you insure contents and to decide in 10 years' time whether that antique chair really was an investment!).

Useful addresses (see *Invaluable phone numbers*, below).

Children (school reports, expense, health, holidays, etc).

Bills and receipts (put them all in here, once paid, until you do your monthly bookkeeping and file them away in their proper places).

To be sorted (anything you haven't yet decided whether or not to keep, but know you want to have another look at: magazine articles, letters, etc).

Your filing cabinet is your own private domain – enjoy it.

Unless you are the hoarding type, keep only the bare minimum of paper – you will never look at most things again.

Invaluable phone numbers

Doctor

Local hospital

Specialist doctors

Nearest 24-hour chemist

Dentist

Vet

Local police station

Insurance broker

Builder

Plumber

Electrician

Gas emergency number

Electricity board

Gas board

Coal or oil supplier

Drain cleaner

Roof repairer

Local town hall

Exterminator

Specialist repairers

Local odd job person

Decorator

Carpenter

Carpet layer

Upholsterer

Gardener

Cleaner

Babysitters

TV/video repairs

Fridge/freezer repairer

Washing machine repairer

Tumble dryer repairer

Dishwasher repairer

Oven/hob repairer

Window cleaner

Laundry

Dry cleaner

Telephone engineers

Newsagents

Local shops that deliver

Florist

Off licence

Favourite restaurants

Local take-aways

Local cinema

Theatre box office

Taxi

AA/RAC emergency

Garage

Railway stations

Coach stations

Airport

Neighbours

Friends (few)

Family

Office(s)

Children's school(s)

Bank

Credit card emergency

Compile your own lists of invaluable phone numbers and keep it by the telephone.

Your important numbers

Passport(s)

Driving licence

Bank account(s)

Credit card(s)

Mortgage policy

Insurance policies

Car registration

National Health

National Insurance

Post Office account

Library card

Club memberships

(AA/RAC)

See also Serial numbers to keep *(page 120).*

Better safe than sorry

Always date letters and make sure addresses and any reference numbers are clearly shown.

Keep copies of all letters you write and receive, apart from personal ones (unless you want to).

Keep a note of the names of people you speak to regarding business, over the telephone; the dates on which you speak and the topics you discussed. It is not only friendlier to remember names, but is more efficient in the long run, and essential if complaining.

Keep all guarantees and receipts, etc safely, and make sure they are dated.

Keep all agreements safely, preferably where you can find them quickly.

Never sign a blank piece of paper or form.

Always fill in cheque stubs so that you can keep tight control over your finances.

Read everything carefully before you sign.

Before employing plumbers, electricians, etc, find out which professional body they belong to, so that if you experience any problems you can always threaten to report them.

Safeguard yourself against loss or theft: note all your numbers now. See *Your important numbers* (page 251).

Dates to go in your diary

Passport renewal date

Visa(s) renewal date(s)

Driving licence renewal date

Vehicle licence(s) renewal date(s)

MOT test date

Resident's Parking Permit renewal date

Next car service

Insurance policies renewal dates

Club memberships

renewal dates (including AA/RAC)

Credit card(s) renewal date(s)

Bank standing orders: note when payments should end and check that the bank has remembered

Dates you pay bills (rates, gas, water, electricity, phone, etc): remember to pay them before you go away on a long holiday

TV licence renewal date

Dog licence renewal date

Doctor's appointments

Next dental appointment: every six months

Any appointments at the vet

Central heating service: yearly

Services for electrical and gas appliances: yearly

Children's holidays

Important gardening dates

Sentimental dates you want to remember

Appointments you have made

Lists to make (and Keep)

Friends' and relations' birthdays and wedding anniversaries. (Try and remember how old they are, and how long they have been married.)

Letters you have to write.

Vital statistics of friends and relations (for buying them clothes), and their favourite perfumes, cigarettes, etc.

Names of people you sent Christmas cards to, and received them from, last year.

People you 'tipped' at Christmas last year, and how much.

Presents you gave and received last year.

Records you want to listen to.

New Year resolutions made, and broken.

People who invited you to dinner, with whom, and what they gave you to eat.

People you invited to dinner, with whom, and what you fed them.

Recipes you want to learn.

Films, plays and concerts you have been to, and your reactions.

Books you want to read.

Books you've read, and what you thought of them.

Words you have come across that you were not sure of, and their meanings.

Places and exhibitions you want to visit.

Measurements of all your rooms and certain pieces of furniture in case you want to buy things for your home.

Weekly shopping.

Things you have got to do tomorrow.

The 'be prepared' bag

Purse (filled)
Cheque-book and cheque card
Credit cards
Change for parking meters and pay phone (for emergencies)
Club membership cards, student or OAP cards, etc
Address book
Diary
Pen and paper (for list-making)
Book
Latest shopping list
Dimensions of all your rooms, furniture, friends, relations, etc, in case you see something you might like to buy them
Keys to home, car, garage, bicycle lock, etc
Shriek alarm (to ward off muggers)
Carrier bag for extra shopping
Make-up
Small mirror
Nail varnish
Nail file
Perfume
Brush and comb
Hair spray
Tissues
Toothpicks and dental floss
Travel toothbrush
Breath freshener

Lip cream
Hand cream
Aspirin
Indigestion tablets
Any medications you
  are taking
Sanitary towels or
  tampons
Prescription glasses
  and case, or
  contact lens case
Card giving any
  important medical
  data

Plasters
Safety pins
Miniature sewing kit
Stain remover
Spare pair of tights or
  stockings, or clear
  nail varnish (for
  stopping ladders)
Jewellery (to brighten
  up your outfit)
Penknife (for most
  emergencies)
Sunglasses
Folding umbrella

When you're bored...

Get your hair cut.

Go swimming.

Invite a new friend round for tea.

Re-plan your garden.

Write a letter about yourself, include some
photographs and send a photo copy to
everyone to whom you owe a letter.

Spoil yourself – have a sauna or massage.

Do all the things you want to do, but never
normally have time to do.

Begin your autobiography.

Attend a lecture or local class.

Visit an elderly friend or relative, and take a
picnic.

Go on a bicycle ride.

Take a day trip to the seaside.

Re-read this book!